Warren Buffett
In His Own Words

Warren Buffett
In His Own Words

EDITED BY
DAVID ANDREWS

AN AGATE IMPRINT

CHICAGO

Printed in the United States.

The Library of Congress has cataloged an earlier edition of this book as follows:

Buffett, Warren.
 The oracle speaks : Warren Buffett in his own words / edited by David
Andrews.
  p. cm. -- (In their own words)
 Includes bibliographical references and index.
 ISBN 978-1-932841-69-5 (pbk.) -- ISBN 1-932841-69-5 (paperback) -- ISBN
978-1-57284-711-8 (ebook)
1. Buffett, Warren--Quotations. 2. Capitalists and financiers--United
States--Biography. 3. Investments--United States. 4. Business--United States.
5. United States--Politics and government. I. Andrews, David. II. Title.
 HG172.B84A3 2012
 332.6--dc23
          2012038354

10 9 8 7 6 5 4 3 2 1   19 20 21 22 23

B2 is an imprint of Agate Publishing. Agate books are available in bulk at
discount prices. For more information, go to agatepublishing.com.

When you get to my age, you'll really measure success in life by how many of the people you want to have love you actually do love you. I know people who have a lot of money, and they get testimonial dinners and they get hospital wings named after them and do all kinds of things. And the truth is that nobody in the world loves them. If you get to my age in life and nobody thinks well of you, I don't care how big your bank account is, it's a disaster.

—**Warren Buffett**

Contents

Introduction

O NE COULD FORGIVE Warren Buffett for lacking in modesty. From his office in Omaha, Nebraska—without even the benefit of a computer—he has racked up an investment record that far surpasses his counterparts on Wall Street, or anyone else in the world, for that matter. While the major stock indexes were gaining about 11 percent a year from the 1950s to the 1990s, Buffett was making investment choices that gained in value by about 29 percent a year, resulting in an investment business—Berkshire Hathaway—that is now the fourth-largest public company in the world, and netting him $84.5 billion.

Yet the Oracle of Omaha speaks modestly of his own abilities. While he acknowledges that he has a unique ability to evaluate businesses, he doesn't feel entitled to the vast wealth that ability has earned him. Instead, he likes to say that he won the "ovarian lottery" by being born with the right skill set, to the right family, at the right place and time. Had he been born a few centuries earlier or somewhere in the developing world, his ability to allocate capital might have been worthless. That's one reason Buffett has pledged to give most of his money to charity, through the Bill and Melinda Gates Foundation as well as foundations run by his three children.

Even though Buffett speaks modestly of himself, he doesn't shy away from the limelight. He is more than willing to expound on his ideas about investment theory, current events, tax policy, or how to live a worthwhile life. He spends hours talking investments on CNBC, pens editorials in the *New York Times*, and shares colloquial stories in his annual report to Berkshire Hathaway shareholders (selections from all of these sources can be found on the following pages).

On investment, Buffett has a few rules. Look for businesses with an "enduring competitive advantage"—ones that could raise their prices tomorrow and not lose customers. Once you find one of those businesses, buy shares if the price is right, and then don't sell. One of the biggest mistakes investors make, he says, is frequently buying and selling stock and paying the broker fees that go with each transaction. That's one reason (besides a personal sense of loyalty) that Berkshire Hathaway rarely sells the stocks it buys, even when the businesses underperform.

Buffett's advice on life is simple, too. Find a profession you love, marry the right person, and love your family unconditionally. Believe in yourself, and don't listen too much to others. It's advice that Buffett has lived throughout his 80-plus years, bringing him not only a vast personal fortune, but more importantly, a loving and joyful life.

Part I

BUSINESS EMPIRE

Investing

RESEARCHING INVESTMENTS

WHEN I BUY a stock, I think of it in terms of buying a whole company just as if I were buying a store down the street. If I were buying the store, I'd want to know all about it.

—Forbes, November 1, 1969

LIMITING YOUR INVESTMENTS

IN THE INVESTMENT world, if you had a punch card when you got out of school, and there were only 20 punches on it, and when that was done, you were all done investing, you'd make more money than having one with unlimited punches. You'd make sure you used them for the right things.

University of Notre Dame, spring 1991

INVESTMENT AND SPORTS

I CALL INVESTING the greatest business in the world, because you never have to swing. You stand at the plate, the pitcher throws you General Motors at 47! U.S. Steel at 39! And nobody calls a strike on you. There's no penalty except for the opportunity lost. All day you wait for the pitch you like; then when the fielders are asleep, you step up and hit it.

—*Forbes*, November 1, 1974

TED WILLIAMS DESCRIBED in his book, *The Science of Hitting*, that the most important thing—for a hitter—is to wait for the right pitch. And that's exactly the philosophy I have about investing. Wait for the right pitch, and wait for the right deal. And it will come. It's the key to investing.

—*CBS News*, February 8, 2012

GAMES ARE WON by players who focus on the playing field—not by those whose eyes are glued to the scoreboard. If you can enjoy Saturdays and Sundays without looking at stock prices, give it a try on weekdays.

—**letter to Berkshire Hathaway shareholders, February 2014**

DEGREE OF DIFFICULTY counts in the Olympics; it doesn't count in business. You don't get any extra points for the fact that something's very hard to do, so you might as well step over one-foot bars rather than try to jump over seven-foot bars.

—**CNBC, October 18, 2010**

The best way to think about investments is to be in a room with no one else and to just think. If that doesn't work, nothing else is going to work.

—University of Florida, October 15, 1998

THE TEMPERAMENT OF AN INVESTOR

SUCCESS IN INVESTING doesn't correlate with IQ once you're above the level of 25. Once you have ordinary intelligence, what you need is the temperament to control the urges that get other people into trouble in investing.

—*BusinessWeek,* July 5, 1999

ORDINARY COMPETENCE, EXTRAORDINARY RESULTS

WHAT WE DO is not beyond anybody else's competence. I feel the same way about managing that I do about investing: It's just not necessary to do extraordinary things to get extraordinary results.

—*Fortune,* April 11, 1988

STUDYING FINANCIAL DATA

If merely looking up past financial data would tell you what the future holds, the Forbes 400 would consist of librarians.

—letter to Berkshire Hathaway shareholders,
February 2009

The unsophisticated investor who is realistic about his shortcomings is likely to obtain better long-term results than the knowledgeable professional who is blind to even a single weakness.

—letter to Berkshire Hathaway shareholders,
February 2014

THE SIMPLICITY OF INVESTMENT

DRAW A CIRCLE around the businesses you understand and then eliminate those that fail to qualify on the basis of value, good management, and limited exposure to hard times.

—*Forbes*, **November 1, 1974**

I DON'T KNOW a thing now that I didn't know at 19 when I read [Benjamin Graham's *The Intelligent Investor*]. For eight years prior to that I was a chartist. I loved all that stuff. I had charts coming out my ears. Then, all of a sudden a fellow explains to me that you don't need all that, just buy something for less than it's worth.

—**University of Notre Dame, spring 1991**

I HAVE THIS complicated procedure I go through every morning, which is to look in the mirror and decide what I'm going to do. And I feel at that point, everybody's had their say.

—*The Snowball*, **2008**

BEATING THE MARKET

THERE IS NO hunch or intuitiveness or anything of the sort. I mean, I try to sit down and figure out what the future economic prospects of a business are.

—**University of Nebraska–Lincoln, October 10, 1994**

HOW DO YOU beat Bobby Fischer? You play him at any game but chess. I try to stay in games where I have an edge.

—*BusinessWeek*, **July 5, 1999**

MOST PEOPLE CAN'T do a couple percentage points better than the market. I'm telling people I still expect to do a little better than average, but nothing like I've done in the past. I wouldn't be running it if I thought I would be doing just average. That may be what happens, and I know that I can't do more than a couple points better than average. But it's better than most people do themselves. It may be better than I do.

—*Haaretz*, **March 23, 2011**

THE ADVANTAGE OF HAVING LESS MONEY

IF I WAS running $1 million today, or $10 million for that matter, I'd be fully invested. Anyone who says that size does not hurt investment performance is selling. The highest rates of return I've ever achieved were in the 1950s. I killed the Dow. You ought to see the numbers. But I was investing peanuts then. It's a huge structural advantage not to have a lot of money. I think I could make you 50 percent a year on $1 million. No, I know I could. I guarantee that.

—*BusinessWeek*, July 5, 1999

IDEA QUOTA

MY IDEA QUOTA used to be like Niagara Falls—I'd have many more than I could use. Now it's as if someone had dammed up the water and was letting it flow with an eyedropper.

—*Forbes*, November 1, 1969

WHEN I GOT started, the bargains were flowing like the Johnstown Flood; by 1969 it was like a leaky toilet in Altoona.

—*Forbes*, November 1, 1974

I BELIEVE IN owning productive assets . . . whether it's farms, apartment houses, or businesses. And they'll do very well over time, and sometimes one class is doing better than another. But if you own any of those things over the next 20 years in the United States, I think you'll do well.

—CNBC, November 14, 2011

WE DON'T WANT to own things where the world is going to change rapidly because I don't think I can see change that well or any better than the next fellow. So, I really want something that I think is going to be quite stable, that has very good economics going for it.

—University of Nebraska–Lincoln, October 10, 1994

The future is never clear; you pay a very high price in the stock market for a cheery consensus. Uncertainty actually is the friend of the buyer of long-term values.

—*Forbes*, August 6, 1979

SPECULATION VS. INVESTMENT

THERE'S NOTHING IMMORAL or illegal or fattening about speculation, but it is an entirely different game to buy a lump of something and hope that somebody else pays you more for that lump two years from now than it is to buy something you expect to produce income for you over time. I bought a farm 30 years ago, not far from here. I've never had a quote on it since. What I do is I look at what it produces every year, and it produces a very satisfactory amount relative to what I paid for it.

—CNBC, March 2, 2011

INVESTING IN VALUE

IF YOU OWN a business, and you plow back a
good portion of your earnings into building
the business, you're going to have something
more valuable on average year after year. Now,
sometimes the market reflects it and sometimes
it's crashing for some other reason or whatever.
But the stock market builds in value, underlying
value, from year to year.

—*Bloomberg Markets*, August 30, 2018

TALK YOURSELF DOWN

THE WHOLE MENTALITY of Wall Street is that if you buy something—even if you're going to buy more of it later on, or if the company is going to buy its own stock in—the people seem to think that they're better off if it goes up the next day, or the next week, or the next month, and that's why they talk about "talking your book."

If we talked our book, from our standpoint, we would say pessimistic things about all four of the biggest holdings we have, because all four of them are repurchasing their shares, and, obviously, the cheaper they repurchase their shares, the better off we are.

—**Berkshire Hathaway annual meeting, May 2, 2015**

REACTING TO UNCERTAINTY

I DO NOT think if Ben Bernanke comes up and whispers to me that he's going to do X, Y, or Z tomorrow, I'm not going to change my view about what businesses I want to own. I want—I'm going to own those businesses for years just like I would own a farm or an apartment house and there'll be all kinds of events and there'll be all kinds of uncertainties and in the end, what will really count is how that business or farm or apartment house does over the years.

—CNBC, November 14, 2011

IF YOUR GOAL is not to manage money in such a way as to get a significantly better return than the world, then I believe in extreme diversification. So I believe 98 or 99 percent of people ... who invest should extensively diversify and not trade, so that leads them to an index fund type of decision with very low costs. All they're going to do is own a part of America and they have made a decision that owning part of America is worthwhile.

—University of Florida, October 15, 1998

IF YOU REALLY know businesses, you probably shouldn't own six of them. If you can identify six wonderful businesses, that is all of the diversification you need, and you're going to make a lot of money, and I will guarantee you that going into a seventh one ... , rather than putting more money into your first one, has got to be a terrible mistake. Very few people have gotten rich on their seventh best idea.

—University of Florida, October 15, 1998

ANYTHING THAT CAUSES people to think they can trade actively in stocks and do better than if they sat on their rear is a terrible mistake. American business has done wonderfully for investors over the years, yet many investors have managed to turn in bad performances. You can say to yourself, if the Dow started the 20th century at 66 and is now at 12,000, how could anybody lose money? But people do lose money. But they lose money by trying to jump in and out of this and that, and think that they should buy this stock because the earnings are going to surprise on the upside or some crazy thing like that. If they just buy good businesses, they'll do fine.

—CNBC, November 14, 2011

ACTIVE TRADING

WALL STREET MAKES its money on activity. You make your money on inactivity. If everybody in this room trades their portfolio around every day with every other person, you're all going to end up broke. The intermediary is going to end up with all the money. On the other hand, if you all own stock in a group of average businesses and just sit here for the next 50 years, you'll end up with a fair amount of money and your broker will be broke.

—University of Florida, October 15, 1998

IF YOU OWN a farm and somebody said, you know, Italy's got problems. Do you sell your farm tomorrow? If you own a good business locally in Omaha and somebody says Italy's got problems tomorrow, do you sell your business? Do you sell your apartment house? No. But for some reason, people think if they own wonderful businesses indirectly through stocks, they've got to make a decision every five minutes.

—CNBC, November 14, 2011

ACTIVE TRADING

(*a*) INVESTORS, OVERALL, will necessarily earn an average return, minus costs they incur; (*b*) Passive and index investors, through their very inactivity, will earn that average minus costs that are very low; (*c*) With that group earning average returns, so must the remaining group—the active investors. But this group will incur high transaction, management, and advisory costs. Therefore, the active investors will have their returns diminished by a far greater percentage than will their inactive brethren. That means that the passive group—the "know-nothings"— must win.

—letter to Berkshire Hathaway shareholders,
February 2008

INVESTING AND THE LAWS OF MOTION

LONG AGO, SIR Isaac Newton gave us three laws of motion, which were the work of genius. But Sir Isaac's talents didn't extend to investing: He lost a bundle in the South Sea Bubble, explaining later, "I can calculate the movement of the stars, but not the madness of men." If he had not been traumatized by this loss, Sir Isaac might well have gone on to discover the Fourth Law of Motion: *For investors as a whole, returns decrease as motion increases.*

—letter to Berkshire Hathaway shareholders,
February 2006

LEARNING HUMAN BEHAVIOR

I LEARNED ENOUGH about investing by the time
I was in my early 20s to take care of me the rest
of my life. . . . But I learned a lot more about
human behavior as I went through life. I did
not learn that by reading a book by Ben Graham
or something where I was going to learn about
investments. I mean, learning about human
behavior, I think, really, 90 percent of is by
experience. I don't think you find a lot of books
that teach you about that.

—Forbes 400 Summit on Philanthropy, June 26, 2012

BUFFETT'S FIRST STOCK

I BOUGHT MY first stock when I was 11. I don't know why I waited so long, I was interested much earlier. But it took me until I was 11 to get the 120 bucks to buy it. I bought three shares of Cities Service, preferred at 38. It went to 27—you remember these things. My sister bought three shares with me. She couldn't stand the idea that I was going to get rich and she wasn't. We would walk to school and she kept reminding me as the stock went down. When it got back up to 40, I sold it. We each made $5 on our three shares. It went to 200 and something afterward. It doesn't pay to talk to your sister about your stocks on the way to school.

—*Georgia Tech Alumni Magazine*, **Winter 2003**

A simple rule dictates my buying: Be fearful when others are greedy, and be greedy when others are fearful.

—*New York Times*, October 16, 2008

USING FEAR

FIRST, WIDESPREAD FEAR is your *friend* as an investor, because it serves up bargain purchases. Second, *personal* fear is your enemy. It will also be unwarranted. Investors who avoid high and unnecessary costs and simply sit for an extended period with a collection of large, conservatively-financed American businesses will almost certainly do well.

—letter to Berkshire Hathaway shareholders,
February 2017

Fear spreads instantaneously. Confidence comes back through the door one at a time.

—Fortune Most Powerful Women Summit,
October 16, 2013

WHEN TO BUY

I TRY TO buy a dollar for 60 cents, and if I think
I can get that, then I don't worry too much
about when. A perfect example of this is British
Columbia Power. In 1962, when it was being
nationalized, everyone knew that the provincial
government was going to pay at least X dollars
and you could buy it for X minus, say, five. As it
turns out, the government paid a lot more.

—*Forbes*, November 1, 1969

IMAGINE IF YOU owned a grocery store and you
had a manic-depressive partner who one day
would offer to sell you his share of the business
for a dollar. Then the next day because the sun
was shining for no reason at all wouldn't sell it
for any price. That's what the market is like and
why you can't buy and sell on its terms. You have
to buy and sell when you want to.

—*Forbes*, November 1, 1969

Don't pass up something that's attractive today because you think you will find something way more attractive tomorrow.

—Columbia University, November 12, 2009

The sillier the market's behavior, the greater the opportunity for the businesslike investor.

—preface, *The Intelligent Investor*, 2003

BUYING TROUBLED COMPANIES

THE BEST THING that happens to us is when a great company gets into temporary trouble.... We want to buy them when they're on the operating table.

—*BusinessWeek*, July 5, 1999

BUYING IN THE BAD TIMES

ON BALANCE, WE will do more business when people are pessimistic. Not because we like pessimism, but because it makes for prices that are much more attractive. If you all have filling stations to sell in South Bend, I want to do business with whomever is most negative about filling stations. And that's where I'm going to make the best buy. Times are really good and times are really bad, over a period of time. We don't quit selling candy in July just because it isn't Christmas.

—University of Notre Dame, spring 1991

Forget what you know about buying fair businesses at wonderful prices; instead, buy wonderful businesses at fair prices.

—letter to Berkshire Hathaway shareholders, February 2015

PRICING STOCKS

IF YOU THINK something is worth a dollar, don't pay 99 cents for it. Buy it at 60 cents so there is a margin of safety. Don't drive up to a bridge that says capacity 10,000 pounds with a 9,900 pound truck and drive across it. Go down the road and find one that says 20,000 pounds.

—*Georgia Tech Alumni Magazine*,
Winter 2003

WHETHER WE'RE TALKING about socks or stocks, I like buying quality merchandise when it is marked down.

—letter to Berkshire Hathaway shareholders,
February 2009

THE MOST IMPORTANT QUESTION

WE NEVER BUY something with a price target
in mind. We never buy something at 30 saying if
it goes to 40 we'll sell it, or 50 or 60 or 100. The
way to look at a business is, is this going to keep
producing more and more money over time? And
if the answer to that is *yes*, you don't need to ask
any more questions.

—University of Florida, October 15, 1998

A BIRD IN THE HAND

AESOP WAS NOT much of a finance major,
because he said something like, "A bird in the
hand is worth two in the bush." But he doesn't say
when.... Sometimes a bird in the hand is better
than two in the bush, and sometimes two in the
bush are better than one in the hand.

—*The Snowball*, 2008

You shouldn't buy a stock, in my view, for any other reason than the fact that you think it's selling for less than it's worth, considering all the factors about the business.

—University of Notre Dame, spring 1991

BUFFETT'S GAS STATION

BACK WHEN I had 10,000 bucks, I put 2,000 of it into a Sinclair service station, which I lost, so my opportunity cost on it's about 6 billion right now. A fairly big mistake—it makes me feel good when Berkshire goes down, because the cost of my Sinclair station goes down too.

—University of Florida, October 15, 1998

BUFFETT'S BIRTH AND THE MARKET

WHEN I WAS born on August 30 of 1930, that was the high day for the whole year—242. It went straight down to 41. My mother must have felt guilty as hell witnessing what had happened.

—*Charlie Rose*, September 30, 2011

Should you find yourself in a chronically leaking boat, energy devoted to changing vessels is likely to be more productive than energy devoted to patching leaks.

—*The Essays of Warren Buffett*, 1997

HYPERVENTILATING AT THE DOW

IT'S AMUSING THAT commentators regularly hyperventilate at the prospect of the Dow crossing an even number of thousands, such as 14,000 or 15,000. If they keep reacting that way, a 5.3 percent annual gain for the century will mean they experience at least 1,986 seizures during the next 92 years.

—letter to Berkshire Hathaway shareholders, February 2008

THE MARKET AS A VOTING MACHINE

IN THE SHORT run [the market] is a voting machine; in the long run it's a weighing machine. Today on Wall Street, they say, "Yes, it's cheap, but it's not going to go up." That's silly. People have been successful investors because they've stuck with successful companies. Sooner or later the market mirrors the business.

—*Forbes*, November 1, 1974

SPLITTING STOCKS

IF SOMEBODY REALLY thinks that the stock is more valuable because we've split it, they're in the wrong show. It's like the guy who went into the pizza parlor and said, "I'd like a pizza." The guy says, "Shall I cut it into four pieces or eight?" And he says, "Better make it four, I couldn't eat eight."

—*Georgia Tech Alumni Magazine*, Winter 2003

UNCERTAINTY

THE WORLD'S ALWAYS uncertain. The world was uncertain on December 6th, 1941, we just didn't know it. The world was uncertain on October 18th, 1987, you know, we just didn't know it. The world was uncertain on September 10th, 2001, we just didn't know it. The world—there's always uncertainty. Now the question is, what do you do with your money? ... If you leave it in your pocket, it'll become worth less—not worthless— worth less over time. That's certain.

—CNBC, November 14, 2011

BONDS

I DO NOT like short-term bonds, and I do not like
long-term bonds. And if you push me, I'm sure
that I don't like intermediate-term bonds either.
I just think it's a terrible mistake to buy into
fixed-dollar investments at these kinds of rates.

—CNBC, March 2, 2011

COMMODITIES

THE PROBLEM WITH commodities is that you're
betting on what somebody else will pay for them
in six months. The commodity itself isn't going to
do anything for you.

—CNBC, March 2, 2011

GOLD IS A way of going along on fear, and it's been a pretty good way of going along on fear from time to time. But you really have to hope people become more afraid in [a] year or two years than they are now. And if they become more afraid you make money, if they become less afraid you lose money. But the gold itself doesn't produce anything.

—CNBC, March 2, 2011

YOU COULD TAKE all the gold that's ever been mined, and it would fill a cube 67 feet in each direction. For what that's worth at current gold prices, you could buy all—not some—all of the farmland in the United States. Plus, you could buy 10 Exxon Mobils, plus have $1 trillion of walking-around money. Or you could have a big cube of metal. Which would you take? Which is going to produce more value?

—CNN, October 19, 2010

ON THE BACK of the US dollar it says, "in god we trust." If Elizabeth Warren were in charge of the government printing office I think it would have to say, "in government we trust," because that is all there is behind paper money. Governments can take actions that decrease the value of money and sometimes at a very, very rapid clip. And I think that's what many people are worried about in this country.

—CNBC, May 2, 2011

CLINGING TO CASH

THOSE INVESTORS WHO cling now to cash are betting they can efficiently time their move away from it later. In waiting for the comfort of good news, they are ignoring Wayne Gretzky's advice: "I skate to where the puck is going to be, not to where it has been."

—*New York Times*, October 16, 2008

RISK AND VOLATILITY

STOCK PRICES WILL always be far more *volatile* than cash-equivalent holdings. *Over the long term*, however, currency-denominated instruments are *riskier* investments—*far* riskier investments—than widely-diversified stock portfolios that are bought over time and that are owned in a manner invoking only token fees and commissions.

—letter to Berkshire Hathaway shareholders,
February 2015

If you and I buy various cryptocurrency they're not gonna multiply. They're not gonna be a bunch of rabbits sitting there in front of us. They're just gonna sit there.

—CNBC, May 7, 2018

TWO INVESTMENT COURSES

I WOULD HAVE a course on how to value a business, and I would have a course on how to think about markets.

And I think if people grasped the basic principles in those two courses that they would be far better off than if they were exposed to a lot of things like modern portfolio theory or option pricing. Who needs option pricing to be in an investment business?

—Berkshire Hathaway annual meeting, May 5, 2012

THE VALUE OF WALL STREET

THE NATURE OF Wall Street is that overall it makes a lot of money relative to the number of people involved, relative to the IQ of the people involved, and relative to the energy expended. They work hard, they're bright, but ... they don't work that much harder or [aren't] that much brighter than somebody that ... is building a dam someplace, you know, or a whole lot of other jobs.

—remarks to the Financial Crisis Inquiry Commission,
May 26, 2010

INVESTORS IN WONDERLAND

MANY HELPERS [INVESTMENT advisors] are apparently direct descendants of the queen in *Alice in Wonderland,* who said: "Why, sometimes I've believed as many as six impossible things before breakfast." Beware the glib helper who fills your head with fantasies while he fills his pockets with fees.

—letter to Berkshire Hathaway shareholders,
February 2008

BAD TERMINOLOGY

BAD TERMINOLOGY IS the enemy of good thinking. When companies or investment professionals use terms such as *EBITDA* or *pro forma,* they want you to unthinkingly accept concepts that are dangerously flawed. (In golf, my score is frequently below par on a *pro forma* basis: I have firm plans to *restructure* my putting stroke and therefore only count the swings I take before reaching the green.)

—letter to Berkshire Hathaway shareholders,
February 2002

You're dealing with a lot of silly people in the marketplace; it's like a great big casino and everyone else is boozing. If you can stick with Pepsi, you should be okay.

—*Forbes*, November 1, 1974

Almost everybody I know in Wall Street has had as many good ideas as I have, they just had a lot of [bad] ideas too.

—University of Notre Dame , spring 1991

THE LURE OF SPECULATION

IT'S ALWAYS POSSIBLE when you get a big asset class that moves on price that after a while, people forget about what the asset class represents and just get entranced with the fact that it went up a lot last week or last month and that their neighbor, who's dumber than they are, had made a lot of money and now their wife is telling them, you know, why aren't you in gold or whatever it may be that's—or Internet stocks.

—CNBC, May 2, 2011

PROFITING FROM BUBBLES

WE DON'T TRY to profit from bubbles. We just try to avoid going broke from them, and so far we've been OK.

—CNBC, May 2, 2011

PEER PRESSURE AND THE CAUSE OF BUBBLES

WHEN YOUR NEIGHBOR has made a lot of money by buying Internet stocks, you know, and your wife says that you're smarter than he is and he's richer than you are, you know, so why aren't you doing it? When that gets to a point, when day trading gets going, all of that sort of thing, very hard to point to what does it.

—remarks to the Financial Crisis Inquiry Commission,
May 26, 2010

ONE MORE BUBBLE

YOU MAY RECALL a 2003 Silicon Valley bumper sticker that implored, "Please, God, Just One More Bubble." Unfortunately, this wish was promptly granted, as just about all Americans came to believe that house prices would forever rise.

—letter to Berkshire Hathaway shareholders,
February 2008

WHEN BUBBLES BURST

W<small>HEN</small> <small>TIMES</small> <small>ARE</small> good, it is kind of like Cinderella at the ball. She knew at midnight that everything was going to turn into pumpkins and mice, but it was just so much damn fun, dancing there, the guys looked better and the drinks got more frequent and there were no clocks on the wall. And that's what happened with capitalism. We have a lot of fun as the bubble blows up, and we all think we are going to get out five minutes before midnight, but there are no clocks on the wall.

—Haaretz, March 23, 2011

EASY MONEY

W<small>HEN</small> <small>PEOPLE</small> <small>THINK</small> there's easy money available they're not inclined to change. Particularly if somebody said a month or two ago, "Watch out for this easy money," and then their neighbors made some more money in the ensuing month or two, it's just—it's overwhelming.

—remarks to the Financial Crisis Inquiry Commission, May 26, 2010

EXCESSIVE LEVERAGE

EXCESSIVE LEVERAGE LEADS to trouble.
Wherever it pops up, not necessarily in the
banking system—it can be in households—but
the idea that you have to leverage yourself to buy
something you can't pay for in its entirety, has its
merits and limitations.

It's kind of like alcohol. One drink is fine, but
10 will get you in a lot of trouble. With leverage,
people have a great propensity to use it because
it's so much fun when it works. There should
be some ways of controlling leverage, and that
applies to individuals with home mortgages.
The idea of people buying houses at 2–3 percent
down is going to lead to trouble.

—*Haaretz*, March 23, 2011

ADDICTIVE LEVERAGE

WHEN LEVERAGE WORKS, it magnifies your gains. Your spouse thinks you're clever, and your neighbors get envious. But leverage is addictive. Once having profited from its wonders, very few people retreat to more conservative practices. And as we all learned in third grade—and some relearned in 2008—any series of positive numbers, however impressive the numbers may be, evaporates when multiplied by a single zero. History tells us that leverage all too often produces zeroes, even when it is employed by very smart people.

—letter to Berkshire Hathaway shareholders,
February 2011

THE DANGER OF LEVERAGE

EXTREME LEVERAGE HAS been, generally speaking, a net minus. The analogy has been made (and there's just enough truth to it to get you in trouble) that in buying some company with enormous amounts of debt, that it's somewhat like driving a car down the road and placing a dagger on the steering wheel pointed at your heart. If you do that, you will be a better driver—that I can assure you. You will drive with unusual care. You also, someday, will hit a small pothole, or a piece of ice, and you will end up gasping. You will have fewer accidents, but when they come along, they'll be fatal.

—**University of Notre Dame, spring 1991**

If you don't have leverage, you don't get into trouble. That's the only way a smart person can go broke. I've always said if you're smart you don't need it and if you're dumb you shouldn't be using it.

—remarks to the Financial Crisis Inquiry Commission, May 26, 2010

LIQUOR, LAYS, AND LEVERAGE

MY PARTNER, CHARLIE, says that there's only three ways that a smart person can go broke. He says, "Liquor, lays, and leverage." Now the truth is the first two he just added because they started with L. It's leverage. And when somebody tells you how they came back and made a second fortune, I'm not impressed, because why the hell would they lose their first fortune?

—CNBC, February 26, 2018

DERIVATIVES

LONG AGO, MARK Twain said: "A man who tries to carry a cat home by its tail will learn a lesson that can be learned in no other way." If Twain were around now, he might try winding up a derivatives business. After a few days, he would opt for cats.

—letter to Berkshire Hathaway shareholders,
February 2006

IF YOU THINK about it, you can't go out and insure my house against fire because you do not have an insurable interest, as they call it in the trade. Because once you insure my house against fire and you may decide that dropping a few matches around my lawn might be a good idea. And credit default swaps, if you don't own underlying debt and you buy a credit default swap, you have an interest in that place getting into trouble.

When a lot of people have an interest in a place getting in trouble, they may start putting out misleading statements about it. I mean, if you were short the stock of a bank, and there wasn't any FDIC, you might go out and hire 100 movie extras to stand in front of that bank. And in effect, you would create your own reality. Now buying credit default swaps and talking about them and causing the price of credit default swaps to go up creates its own reality to some degree.

—CNBC, November 14, 2011

Berkshire Hathaway

The big money— huge money— is in selling people the idea that you can do something magical for them.

Borkshire Hathaway annual meeting,
May 6, 2017

If I can make one good decision a year, you know, we'll do OK.

—*CBS News*, February 8, 2012

THE IMPORTANCE OF A GOOD DECISION

WHEN I MAKE the decisions at Berkshire, I'm thinking about the fact that I've got 99 percent of my net worth in it and it's all going to charities, so, I mean, if I cause this place to go broke, there's a lot of downside to me.

—remarks to the Financial Crisis Inquiry Commission,
May 26, 2010

OWN, DON'T BORROW

WE NEVER GET out on a limb rod. We always have lots of money. We never borrow a lot of money.

—CNN Business, December 26, 2012

Up until a few years ago, we sold things to buy more because I ran out of money. I had more ideas than money. Now I have more money than ideas.

—*BusinessWeek*, July 5, 1999

STUDYING FAILURE

I LIKE TO study failure, actually. My partner says, "All I want to know is where I'll die so I'll never go there." And we want to see what has caused businesses to go bad—and the biggest thing that kills them is complacency. You want a restlessness, a feeling, you know, that somebody's always after you, but you're going to stay ahead of them. You always want to be on the move.

—Coca-Cola annual meeting, April 24, 2013

NEVER LOOKING BACK

WE NEVER LOOK back. You know, we just figure there's so much to look forward to, there's no sense thinking about what we might have—it just doesn't make any difference. I mean, you can only live life forward.

—University of Florida, October 15, 1998

MAKING MISTAKES

MISTAKES DON'T BOTHER me. I try to never do anything that would jeopardize the well-being of the whole place. So I build into the decisions I make the fact that I am going to make mistakes.

—*Haaretz*, March 23, 2011

I'LL MAKE MORE mistakes in the future—you can bet on that. A line from Bobby Bare's country song explains what too often happens with acquisitions: "I've never gone to bed with an ugly woman, but I've sure woke up with a few."

—letter to Berkshire Hathaway shareholders,
February 2008

MISTAKES OF OMISSION

I'VE MADE ALL kinds of huge mistakes of
omission. The ones of commission show up
in accounting. If I buy something for $1 and
sell it for 50 cents, it shows up.... We've made
relatively minor mistakes of commission.
Those aren't the ones that bother me. The acts
of omission that I'm talking about are things
within my circle of confidence, things I could
understand, did understand, and didn't do
anything about. I was sucking my thumb. Those
are the big mistakes.

—*Georgia Tech Alumni Magazine*, Winter 2003

That old line, "The other guy is doing it, so we must as well," spells trouble in any business.

—letter to Berkshire Hathaway shareholders,
February 2014

MAKING MONEY TOGETHER

WE WANT TO make money only when our partners do and in exactly the same proportion. Moreover, when I do something dumb, I want you to be able to derive some solace from the fact that my financial suffering is proportional to yours.

—*The Essays of Warren Buffett*, 1997

MAKING SHAREHOLDERS RICH

OUR SHAREHOLDERS ARE *far* wealthier today than they would be if the funds we used for acquisitions had instead been devoted to share repurchases or dividends.

—letter to Berkshire Hathaway shareholders, March 2013

STRUCTURING DEALS

IF I WERE to buy a farm and have someone run it for me, the deal I would make with the farmer in terms of what percentage of the crop he would get would be important. If I had someone managing an apartment building for me, my arrangement with him is important. It's important not only in terms of how the profits will be shared, it's important in assessing the person's attitude. You want someone running a place that looks at you as a partner and not as an adversary, and at Berkshire Hathaway, we really look at our shareholders as partners.

—*Haaretz*, March 23, 2011

I have a friend that used to like to own 100 percent of any company that he had, because he liked to look in the mirror and say, "All my shareholders love me." That has a nice ring to it. I like to look in the mirror and say, "Enough of my shareholders love me."

—Fortune Most Powerful Women Summit,
October 16, 2013

OVERSEEING BERKSHIRE'S BUSINESSES

WE WILL NEVER allow Berkshire to become some monolith that is overrun with committees, budget presentations, and multiple layers of management. Instead, we plan to operate as a collection of separately-managed medium-sized and large businesses, most of whose decision-making occurs at the operating level.

—**letter to Berkshire Hathaway shareholders,
February 2010**

HOLDING ON TO BUSINESSES

I DON'T LIKE to sell. We buy everything with the idea that we will hold them forever.... That's the kind of shareholder I want with me in Berkshire. I've never had a target price or a target holding period on a stock. And I have enormous reluctance to sell our wholly owned businesses under almost any circumstances.

—*BusinessWeek*, **July 5, 1999**

ONE BIG SAVINGS ACCOUNT

BERKSHIRE, IN EFFECT, for 53 years, has been a savings account.... Charlie put his money in, I put my money in.... And it's a way of saving money over time. And the money gets left in, and we invest it.

—CNBC, February 26, 2018

SELLING SUBPAR BUSINESSES

REGARDLESS OF PRICE, we have no interest at all in selling any good businesses that Berkshire owns. We are also very reluctant to sell subpar businesses as long as we expect them to generate at least some cash and as long as we feel good about their managers and labor relations.... Gin rummy managerial behavior (discard your least promising business at each turn) is not our style. We would rather have our overall results penalized a bit than engage in that kind of behavior.

—*The Essays of Warren Buffett*, 1997

Unlike [leveraged buyout] operators and private equity firms, we have no "exit" strategy—we buy to keep. That's one reason why Berkshire is usually the first—and sometimes the only—choice for sellers and their managers.

—letter to Berkshire Hathaway shareholders,
February 2003

THE FIRST CALL

FOR SOMEBODY THAT cares about a business that they and their parents and maybe their grandparents lovingly built over decades—if they care about where that business ends up being after, for one reason or another, they don't want to keep it or can't keep it in the family, we absolutely are the first call.

—Berkshire Hathaway annual meeting, May 5, 2018

DON'T SELL A GOOD BUSINESS

WHEN PEOPLE COME to me with wonderful businesses, and they do, and they talk about selling them to me, my first advice is, don't sell them. I mean, wonderful businesses, they're too rare. And if you've got one in your family, keep it unless something forces you to sell it.

—Fortune Most Powerful Women Summit,
October 16, 2013

BERKSHIRE'S CONGREGATION

IF I HAD a church and I was the preacher, and half the congregation left every Sunday, I wouldn't say, "Oh, this is marvelous, because I have all this liquidity among all my members! There's terrific turnover!" I would rather get a church where all the seats were filled every Sunday by the same people. Well that's the same way we look at the businesses we buy. We want to buy something that we're really happy to own virtually forever.

—University of Florida, October 15, 1998

PAYING BERKSHIRE'S DIRECTORS

AT BERKSHIRE, WANTING our fees to be
meaningless to our directors, we pay them
only a pittance. Additionally, not wanting to
insulate our directors from any corporate
disaster we might have, we don't provide them
with officers' and directors' liability insurance
(an unorthodoxy that, not so incidentally, has
saved our shareholders many millions of dollars
over the years). Basically, we want the behavior
of our directors to be driven by the effect their
decisions will have on their family's net worth,
not by their compensation

—letter to Berkshire Hathaway shareholders,
February 2003

INSTITUTIONAL FAILURE AND CEO COMPENSATION

YOU WILL ALWAYS have institutions too big to fail, and sometimes they will fail in the next 100 years. But you will have fewer failures if the person on top and the board of directors who select that person and who set the terms of his or her employment if they have a lot to lose.

—remarks to the Financial Crisis Inquiry Commission,
May 26, 2010

INFLATING CEOS

NOBODY KNOWS IN business whether you're batting .320 or not so everybody says they're a .320 hitter. And the board of directors has to say, well, we've got a .320 hitter, because they couldn't be responsible for picking a guy that bats .250.

—remarks to the Financial Crisis Inquiry Commission,
May 26, 2010

THE QUALITIES OF A GOOD DIRECTOR

THE CURRENT CRY is for "independent" directors. It is certainly true that it is desirable to have directors who think and speak independently—but they must also be business-savvy, interested, and shareholder-oriented....

Over a span of 40 years, I have been on 19 public-company boards (excluding Berkshire's) and have interacted with perhaps 250 directors. Most of them were "independent" as defined by today's rules. But the great majority of these directors lacked at least one of the three qualities I value. As a result, their contribution to shareholder well-being was minimal at best and, too often, negative. These people, decent and intelligent though they were, simply did not know enough about business and/or care enough about shareholders to question foolish acquisitions or egregious compensation.

—letter to Berkshire Hathaway shareholders,
February 2003

The CEO job self-selects for "can-do" types. If Wall Street analysts or board members urge that brand of CEO to consider possible acquisitions, it's a bit like telling your ripening teenager to be sure to have a normal sex life.

—letter to Berkshire Hathaway shareholders,
February 2018

ABCS OF BUSINESS DECAY

MY SUCCESSOR WILL need one other particular strength: the ability to fight off the ABCs of business decay, which are arrogance, bureaucracy and complacency. When these corporate cancers metastasize, even the strongest of companies can falter.

—letter to Berkshire Hathaway shareholders,
February 2015

HOW NOT TO CHOOSE DIRECTORS

CONSULTANTS AND CEOs seeking board candidates will often say, "We're looking for a woman," or "a Hispanic," or "someone from abroad," or what have you. It sometimes sounds as if the mission is to stock Noah's ark. Over the years I've been queried many times about potential directors and have yet to hear *anyone* ask, "Does he think like an intelligent owner?"

—letter to Berkshire Hathaway shareholders,
February 2007

OVERPAYING CEOS

IT'S DIFFICULT TO overpay the *truly* extraordinary CEO of a giant enterprise. But this species is rare. Too often, executive compensation in the United States is ridiculously out of line with performance. That won't change, moreover, because the deck is stacked against investors when it comes to the CEO's pay.

The upshot is that a mediocre-or-worse CEO—aided by his handpicked VP of human relations and a consultant from the ever-accommodating firm of Ratchet, Ratchet, and Bingo—all too often receives gobs of money from an ill-designed compensation arrangement.

—letter to Berkshire Hathaway shareholders,
February 2006

I AM THE compensation committee for 70-some companies which Berkshire owns. It's not rocket science. And we pay a lot of money to some of our CEOs, but it's all performance. When they make a lot of money it's performance related. And we have different arrangements for different people. But we've never hired a compensation consultant, ever. And we never will. If I don't know enough to figure out the compensation for these people, you know, somebody else should be in my job.

—remarks to the Financial Crisis Inquiry Commission,
May 26, 2010

REPLACING CEOS

IT'S ALMOST IMPOSSIBLE ... in a boardroom populated by well-mannered people, to raise the question of whether the CEO should be replaced. It's equally awkward to question a proposed acquisition that has been endorsed by the CEO, particularly when his inside staff and outside advisors are present and unanimously support his decision. (They wouldn't be in the room if they didn't.) Finally, when the compensation committee—armed, as always, with support from a high-paid consultant—reports on a megagrant of options to the CEO, it would be like belching at the dinner table for a director to suggest that the committee reconsider.

—letter to Berkshire Hathaway shareholders,
February 2003

CEOS AND NEGATIVE REINFORCEMENT

THERE SHOULD BE more downside to the head of any institution that has to go to the federal government to be saved for reasons of the greater society. And so far, we have been better at carrots [than] sticks in rewarding CEOs at the top. But I think some more sticks are called for.

—Columbia University, November 12, 2009

CEO PERKS

YOU'VE READ LOADS about CEOs who have received astronomical compensation for mediocre results. Much less well-advertised is the fact that America's CEOs also generally live the good life. Many, it should be emphasized, are exceptionally able, and almost all work far more than 40 hours a week. But they are usually treated like royalty in the process. (And we're certainly going to keep it that way at Berkshire. Though Charlie still favors sackcloth and ashes, I prefer to be spoiled rotten. Berkshire owns the Pampered Chef; our wonderful office group has made me the Pampered Chief.)

—letter to Berkshire Hathaway shareholders,
February 2007

CEO PERKS

HUGE SEVERANCE PAYMENTS, lavish perks and outsized payments for ho-hum performance often occur because comp committees have become slaves to comparative data. The drill is simple: Three or so directors—*not chosen by chance*—are bombarded for a few hours before a board meeting with pay statistics that perpetually ratchet upwards. Additionally, the committee is told about new perks that other managers are receiving. In this manner, outlandish goodies are showered upon CEOs simply because of a corporate version of the argument we all used when children: "But, Mom, all the other kids have one." When comp committees follow this "logic," yesterday's most egregious excess becomes today's baseline.

—letter to Berkshire Hathaway shareholders,
February 2006

MANAGERS THINKING LIKE OWNERS

I LIKE GUYS who forget that they sold the business to me and run the show like proprietors. When I marry their daughter, she continues to live with her parents.

—*Wall Street Journal*, March 31, 1977

WE HAVE A business with very few rules. The only rules the managers have is to basically think like owners. We want those people thinking exactly like they own those businesses themselves. Psychologically, we don't even want them to think there is a Berkshire Hathaway.

—**University of Notre Dame, spring 1991**

We are not in the business of trying to change people. We don't try and change people when we buy the entire business. We think it's like marrying somebody to change them. It just doesn't work very well.

—Berkshire Hathaway annual meeting, May 5, 2012

BERKSHIRE'S MANAGERS

IN 38 YEARS, we've never had a single CEO of a subsidiary elect to leave Berkshire to work elsewhere. Counting Charlie, we now have six managers over 75, and I hope that in four years that number increases by at least two (Bob Shaw and I are both 72). Our rationale: It's hard to teach a new dog old tricks.

—letter to Berkshire Hathaway shareholders,
February 2003

USING SMART PEOPLE

I DON'T HAVE to be smart about everything; I didn't deliver my wife's baby! So, I believe in using people who are smarter than I am.

—*Forbes India*, April 20, 2011

MY MANAGERIAL MODEL is Eddie Bennett, who was a batboy. In 1919, at age 19, Eddie began his work with the Chicago White Sox, who that year went to the World Series. The next year, Eddie switched to the Brooklyn Dodgers, and they, too, won their league title. Our hero, however, smelled trouble.

Changing boroughs, he joined the Yankees in 1921, and they promptly won their first pennant in history. Now Eddie settled in, shrewdly seeing what was coming. In the next seven years, the Yankees won five American League titles. What does this have to do with management? It's simple—to be a winner, work with winners.

—letter to Berkshire Hathaway shareholders,
February 2003

COST-CONSCIOUSNESS

WE CHERISH COST-CONSCIOUSNESS at Berkshire. Our model is the widow who went to the local newspaper to place an obituary notice. Told there was a 25-cents-a-word charge, she requested "Fred Brown died." She was then informed there was a seven-word minimum. "Okay," the bereaved woman replied, "make it 'Fred Brown died, golf clubs for sale.'"

—letter to Berkshire Hathaway shareholders, February 2003

CUTTING COSTS

WHENEVER I READ about some company undertaking a cost-cutting program, I know it's not a company that really knows what costs are all about. Spurts don't work in this area. The really good manager does not wake up in the morning and say, "This is the day I'm going to cut costs," any more than he wakes up and decides to practice breathing.

—*Fortune*, April 11, 1988

I believe enormously in efficiency. I mean, it's the only way living improves, is to get more output per unit of input.

—CNBC, February 29, 2016

WE'VE READ MANAGEMENT treatises that specify exactly how many people should report to any one executive, but they make little sense to us. When you have able managers of high character running businesses about which they are passionate, you can have a dozen or more reporting to you and still have time for an afternoon nap. Conversely, if you have even one person reporting to you who is deceitful, inept or uninterested, you will find yourself with more than you can handle. Charlie and I could work with double the number of managers we now have, so long as they had the rare qualities of the present ones.

—*The Essays of Warren Buffett,* 1997

BE CAREFUL WITH INCENTIVES

YOU REALLY HAVE to be very careful in the messages you send as a CEO. . . . If you tell your managers you never want to disappoint Wall Street, and you want to report X per share, you may find that they start fudging figures to protect your predictions.

—Berkshire Hathaway annual meeting, May 2, 2015

LETTING MANAGERS MANAGE

USUALLY THE MANAGERS [we hire] came with the companies we bought, having demonstrated their talents throughout careers that spanned a wide variety of business circumstances. They were managerial stars long before they knew us, and our main contribution has been to not get in their way. This approach seems elementary: if my job were to manage a golf team—and if Jack Nicklaus or Arnold Palmer were willing to play for me—neither would get a lot of directives from me about how to swing.

—*The Essays of Warren Buffett*, 1997

LETTING MANAGERS MANAGE

THERE ARE MANY giant company managers whom I greatly admire; Ken Chenault of American Express, Jeff Immelt of GE and Dick Kovacevich of Wells Fargo come quickly to mind. But I don't think I could do the management job they do. And I know I wouldn't enjoy many of the duties that come with their positions—meetings, speeches, foreign travel, the charity circuit, and governmental relations. For me, Ronald Reagan had it right: "It's probably true that hard work never killed anyone—but why take the chance?"

—**letter to Berkshire Hathaway shareholders, February 2007**

WE CAN FREE managers up. I would say that we might very well free up at least 20 percent of the time of a CEO in the normal public . . . company— just in terms of meeting with analysts, and the calls, and dealing with banks, and all kinds of things that, essentially, we relieve them of so that they can spend all of their time figuring out the best way to run their business.

—**Berkshire Hathaway annual meeting, May 6, 2017**

When a manager with a reputation for brilliance meets up with a business with a reputation for bad economics, it's the reputation of the business that remains intact.

—CNBC, October 18, 2010

[Jay-Z is] a real business man. I'm just pretending.

—*New York Times*, October 18, 2011

HIRING

WE DON'T HIRE because we get a tax break or because someone in the government tells us to. We hire when there's more demand for what we are making or moving or selling. It's that simple.

—CNN, October 19, 2010

ENJOYING WORK

I HAVE CREATED something that I enjoy.... It's a little crazy, it seems to me, if you are building a business and creating a business, not to create something you are going to enjoy when you get through. It's like painting a painting. I mean, you ought to paint something you are going to enjoy looking at when you get through.

—University of Nebraska–Lincoln, October 10, 1994

Other

Businesses

If we have a strength, it is in recognizing when we are operating well within our circle of competence and when we are approaching the perimeter.

—letter to Berkshire Hathaway shareholders,
March 2000

PRICING POWER

THE SINGLE MOST important decision in evaluating a business is pricing power. You've got the power to raise prices without losing the business to a competitor, and you've got a very good business. And if you have to have a prayer session before raising the price by a tenth of a cent, then you've got a terrible business.

—remarks to the Financial Crisis Inquiry Commission,
May 26, 2010

A TRULY GREAT business must have an enduring *moat* that protects excellent returns on invested capital. The dynamics of capitalism guarantee that competitors will repeatedly assault any business *castle* that is earning high returns. Therefore a formidable barrier such as a company's being the low-cost producer (GEICO, Costco) or possessing a powerful world-wide brand (Coca-Cola, Gillette, American Express) is essential for sustained success. Business history is filled with *Roman candles*, companies whose moats proved illusory and were soon crossed.

—letter to Berkshire Hathaway shareholders,
February 2008

UNDERSTANDING A BUSINESS

WE DON'T DO due diligence or go out kicking tires. It doesn't matter. What matters is understanding the competitive dynamics of a business. We can't be taken by a guy with a sales pitch. ... What really counts is the presence of a competitive advantage. You want a business with a big castle and a moat around it, and you want that moat to widen over time.

—*BusinessWeek*, July 5, 1999

MY JOB IS to look at the universe of things I can understand—I can understand Ike Friedman's jewelry store—and then I try to figure what that stream of cash, in and out, is going to be over a period of time, just like we did with See's Candies, and discounting that back at an appropriate rate, which would be the long-term government rate. [Then] I try to buy it at a price that is significantly below that. And that's about it. Theoretically, I'm doing that with all the businesses in the world—those that I can understand.

—University of Notre Dame, spring 1991

We do no due diligence. My due diligence is to look into their eyes, basically.

—Fortune Most Powerful Women Summit,
October 13, 2015

A CAPITAL BUSINESS

WE WENT INTO department stores—but we didn't think of ourselves as department store guys, or we didn't think of ourselves as steel guys, or tire guys, or anything of that sort.

So we've thought of ourselves as having capital to allocate. If you start with a given industry focus and you spend your whole time working on a way to make a better tire, or whatever it may be, I think it's hard to have the flexibility of mind that you have if you just think you have a large—hopefully large—and growing pile of capital, and trying to figure out what is the . . . best next move that you can make with that capital. And I think we do have a real advantage that way.

—Berkshire Hathaway annual meeting, April 30, 2016

DON'T BE A HORSE

WE ARE FREE of historical biases created by lifelong association with a given industry and are not subject to pressures from colleagues having a vested interest in maintaining the status quo. That's important: If horses had controlled investment decisions, there would have been no auto industry.

—letter to Berkshire Hathaway shareholders,
February 2015

DELIGHT THE CUSTOMER

YOU NEED A genuine desire, day in, day out, to delight the customer. I've never seen a business— and I've seen a lot of businesses—but I've never seen one that delights the customer that doesn't succeed.

—Goldman Sachs 10,000 Small Businesses Summit,
February 13, 2018

PREMIUM BUSINESSES

WALK THROUGH A supermarket sometime and
think about who's got pricing power, and who's
got a franchise, and who doesn't. If you go buy
Oreo cookies, and I'm going to take home Oreo
cookies or something that looks like Oreo cookies
for the kids, or your spouse, or whomever, you'll
buy the Oreo cookies. If the other is three cents a
package cheaper, you'll still buy the Oreo cookies.
... But, if you go to buy milk, it doesn't make any
difference whether it's Borden's, or Sealtest, or
whatever. And you will not pay a premium to
buy one milk over another.... It's the difference
between having a wonderful business and not a
wonderful business. The milk business is not a
good business.

—**University of Notre Dame, spring 1991**

THE NAME *AMERICAN EXPRESS* is one of the
greatest franchises in the world. Even with
terrible management it was bound to make
money.

—*Forbes*, **November 1, 1969**

Buy stock in a business that's so good that an idiot can run it, because sooner or later one will.

—Fortune Most Powerful Women Summit,
October 7, 2014

CAPITAL-INTENSIVE BUSINESSES

IF YOU HAVE a choice between going to work
for a wonderful business that is not capital
intensive, and one that is capital intensive, I
suggest that you look at the one that is not capital
intensive.

—University of Notre Dame, spring 1991

NEWSPAPERS

LET'S FACE IT—NEWSPAPERS are a hell of a lot
more interesting a business than, say, making
couplers for rail cars. While I don't get involved
in the editorial operations of the papers I own,
I really enjoy being part of the institutions that
help shape society.

—*Wall Street Journal*, March 31, 1977

The world isn't going to tell you about great deals. You have to find them yourself.

—Columbia University, November 12, 2009

THE SCUTTLEBUTT APPROACH

I DID A lot of work in the earlier years just in
getting familiar with businesses. The way I
would do that is I would go out and use what Phil
Fisher called the *scuttlebutt approach*. I'd go out,
I'd talk to customers, I'd talk to ex-employees in
some cases, I'd talk to suppliers—everybody....
Let's say I was interested in the coal industry.
I'd go out and see every coal company and I'd
ask every CEO, "If you were to only buy stock in
one coal company that wasn't your own, which
would it be and why?" And you piece those things
together and you learn a lot about the business
after a while.

—**University of Florida, October 15, 1998**

I read hundreds of annual reports every year. I don't talk to any brokers—I don't want to talk to brokers. People are not going to give you great ideas.

—University of Notre Dame, spring 1991

THE IMPORTANT THING is to know what you know and know what you don't know. If you can extend the field of things that you know then so much the better. Obviously, if you understand a great number of businesses, then you have a better chance of succeeding than if you only understand a few.

The important thing is to know the perimeter of your circle of confidence and to play within that circle—the bigger the better. But if something isn't within my circle, I'm not going to be in that game. I found out about this Norwegian chess champion who's 20 years old. At 80 you would think that I'm better than him, but I'm not, and if I play him, he is going to beat me. He is going to beat me in about three moves.

—*Haaretz*, **March 23, 2011**

GROWTH VS. PROFITS

CHARLIE AND I avoid businesses whose futures we can't evaluate, no matter how exciting their products may be. In the past, it required no brilliance for people to foresee the fabulous growth that awaited such industries as autos (in 1910), aircraft (in 1930), and television sets (in 1950). But the future then also included competitive dynamics that would decimate almost all of the companies entering those industries. Even the survivors tended to come away bleeding. . . . At Berkshire we will stick with businesses whose profit picture for decades to come seems reasonably predictable.

—letter to Berkshire Hathaway shareholders,
February 2010

BUYING COMPANIES VS. STOCKS

CHARLIE AND I look for companies that have (*a*) a business we understand; (*b*) favorable long-term economics; (*c*) able and trustworthy management; and (*d*) a sensible price tag. We like to buy the whole business or, if management is our partner, at least 80 percent. When control-type purchases of quality aren't available, though, we are also happy to simply buy small portions of great businesses by way of stock-market purchases. It's better to have a part interest in the Hope Diamond than to own all of a rhinestone.

—letter to Berkshire Hathaway shareholders,
February 2008

LOOKING FOR "ELEPHANTS"

THE UNIVERSE I can't play in [i.e., small companies] has become more attractive than the universe I can play in [large companies]. I have to look for elephants. It may be that the elephants are not as attractive as the mosquitoes. But that is the universe I must live in.

—*BusinessWeek,* July 5, 1999

CASH IS OUR favorite medium of purchase just because we're going to generate a lot of it. And we hate giving out shares.

We do not like the idea of trading away part of See's Candies or GEICO or ISCAR or BNSF. The idea of leaving you with a lower percentage interest in those companies because of any acquisition ambitions of ours is anathema to us.

—Berkshire Hathaway annual meeting,
May 5, 2012

AVOIDING START-UPS

WE HAVE NEVER, that I can think of, bought into start-ups or anything of the sort. . . . I love what they're coming up with, but I don't bring anything to that game at all. And the valuations tend to be, you know, nosebleed by our standards. I want to buy very big, very solid businesses that I know will be around for 50 or 100 years, and buy them at a reasonable price, have a manager run them, and then just, you know, go back to drinking Coca-Cola and eating some peanuts.

—Fortune Most Powerful Women Summit,
October 13, 2015

SEE'S CANDY

OUR SEE'S CANDY is now $11 a pound thanks to my brilliance.... Let's say there's candy available at $6 a pound. Do you really want to walk in on Valentine's Day and hand—I mean your wife has all these favorable images of See's candies over the years, ... and say, "Honey, this year I took the low bid," and then hand her a box of candy? It just isn't going to work.

—University of Florida, October 15, 1998

COCA-COLA AND HAPPINESS

COCA-COLA IS ASSOCIATED with people being happy around the world ...: Disneyland or Disney World, at the World Cup, or at the Olympics— every place that people are happy. Happiness and Coke go together. Now you give me—I don't care how much money—and tell me that I'm going to do that with RC Cola around the world and have 5 billion people that have a favorable image about RC Cola? You can't get it done.... And that's what you want to have in a business.

—University of Florida, October 15, 1998

THE TASTE OF COLAS

COLA HAS NO taste memory. You can drink one of these at nine o' clock, eleven o' clock, three o' clock, five o' clock—the one at five o' clock will taste just as good to you as the one you drank earlier in the morning. You can't do that with cream soda, root beer, orange, grape—you name it. All of those things accumulate on you.... You get sick of them after a while.... And that means that you get people around the world that are heavy users, that will drink five a day or [with] Diet Coke maybe seven or eight a day or something of the sort. They'll never do that with other products, so you get this incredible per capita consumption.

—University of Florida, October 15, 1998

HERSHEY'S

IF YOU WALK into a drugstore, and you say "I'd like a Hershey bar" and the man says "I don't have any Hershey bars, but I've got this unmarked chocolate bar, and it's a nickel cheaper than a Hershey bar," you just go across the street and buy a Hershey bar. *That* is a good business.

University of Notre Dame, spring 1991

GILLETTE

GILLETTE IS MARVELOUS. Gillette supplies over 60 percent of the dollar value of razor blades in the world. When I go to bed at night and I think of all those billions of males sitting there with their hair growing on their faces while I sleep, that can put you to sleep very comfortably.

—University of Nebraska–Lincoln,
October 10, 1994

THE DAILY RACING FORM

THE HIGHEST PRICED daily newspaper in the
United States, with any circulation at all, is the
Daily Racing Form. It sells about 150,000 copies
a day, and it has for about 50 years, and it's either
$2.00 or $2.25 (they keep raising prices) and it's
essential. If you're heading to the racetrack and
you've got a choice between ... Joe's Little Green
Sheet, and the *Daily Racing Form*, if you're a
serious racing handicapper, you want the *Form*.
You can charge $2.00 for the *Form*, you can
charge $1.50, you can charge $2.50, and people
are going to buy it. It's like selling needles to
addicts, basically. It's an essential business.

—**University of Notre Dame, spring 1991**

THE WALT DISNEY COMPANY

LOOK AT WHAT Walt Disney was worth on the
stock market in the first half of 1966. The price
per share was $53, and this didn't look especially
cheap, but on that basis you could buy the whole
company for $80 million when *Snow White*,
Swiss Family Robinson, and some other cartoons,
which had been written off the books, were worth
that much. And then you had Disneyland and
Walt Disney, a genius, as a partner.

—*Forbes*, November 1, 1969

THE WALT DISNEY COMPANY

WE BOUGHT 5 percent of the Walt Disney Company in 1966. It cost us four million dollars. Eighty million bucks was the valuation of the whole thing. . . .

There were no residual values placed on the value of any Disney picture up through the '60s. So [you got all of this] for eighty million bucks, and you got Walt Disney to work for you. It was incredible. . . . And the reason was, in 1966 people said, "Well, *Mary Poppins* is terrific this year, but they're not going to have another *Mary Poppins* next year, so the earnings will be down." I don't care if the earnings are down like that. You know you've still got *Mary Poppins* to throw out in seven more years, assuming kids squawk a little. I mean there's no better system than to have something where, essentially, you get a new crop every seven years and you get to charge more each time.

—University of Notre Dame, spring 1991

MAKING MONEY FROM THE INTERNET

THE INTERNET AS a phenomenon is just huge. That much I understand. I just don't know how to make money at it.... I don't try to profit from the Internet. But I do want to understand the damage it can do to an established business. Our approach is very much profiting from lack of change rather than from change. With Wrigley chewing gum, it's the lack of change that appeals to me. I don't think it is going to be hurt by the Internet. That's the kind of business I like.

—*BusinessWeek,* July 5, 1999

THE HYPE OF INTERNET COMPANIES

THE INTERNET WAS going to change our lives, but it didn't mean that every company was worth $50 billion that could dream up a prospectus.

—remarks to the Financial Crisis Inquiry Commission, May 26, 2010

TEXTILES

OUR TEXTILE BUSINESS—THAT'S a business that took me 22 years to figure out it wasn't very good. Well, in the textile business, we made over half of the men's suit linings in the United States. If you wore a men's suit, chances were that it had a Hathaway lining. And we made them during World War II, when customers couldn't get their linings from other people. Sears Roebuck voted us Supplier of the Year. They were wild about us. The thing was, they wouldn't give us another half a cent a yard because nobody had ever gone into a men's clothing store and asked for a pin striped suit with a Hathaway lining. You just don't see that.

—**University of Notre Dame, spring 1991**

THREE SUGGESTIONS FOR investors: First,
beware of companies displaying weak
accounting.... When managements take the low
road in aspects that are visible, it is likely they
are following a similar path behind the scenes....

Second, unintelligible footnotes usually
indicate untrustworthy management. If you
can't understand a footnote or other managerial
explanation, it's usually because the CEO doesn't
want you to. Enron's descriptions of certain
transactions *still* baffle me.

Finally, be suspicious of companies that
trumpet earnings projections and growth
expectations. Businesses seldom operate in a
tranquil, no-surprise environment, and earnings
simply don't advance smoothly (except, of
course, in the offering books of investment
bankers).... Managers that always promise
to "make the numbers" will at some point be
tempted to *make up* the numbers.

> —letter to Berkshire Hathaway shareholders,
> February 2003

In the world of business, bad news often surfaces serially: You see a cockroach in your kitchen; as the days go by, you meet his relatives.

—letter to Berkshire Hathaway shareholders,
February 2015

SOMETHING WRONG EVERYWHERE

WE'VE GOT, I don't know how many, 30 companies we own stock in or something like that. I will guarantee you there's something going wrong at almost every one of them. I mean, it's not my job to run those companies. It is my job to determine, when something goes wrong, whether it's going to be permanent.

—CNN Business, November 11, 2010

RISK AND HUMAN NATURE

AS LONG AS human beings run institutions, including financial institutions, there will be people that take undue risks, there will sometimes be people that steal, there will be—you know, there will be people that don't understand the risks they're taking. It's just the nature of business.

—CNBC, November 14, 2011

You only learn who has been swimming naked when the tide goes out.

—letter to Berkshire Hathaway shareholders, February 2008

THE HIGH ROAD IN CORPORATE AMERICA

FORMER SENATOR ALAN Simpson famously said: "Those who travel the high road in Washington need not fear heavy traffic." If he had sought truly deserted streets, however, the Senator should have looked to Corporate America's accounting.

—letter to Berkshire Hathaway shareholders, February 2008

INFLATED EARNINGS

FOR MANY YEARS, I've had little confidence in the earnings numbers reported by most corporations. I'm not talking about Enron and WorldCom—examples of outright crookedness. Rather, I am referring to the legal, but improper, accounting methods used by chief executives to inflate reported earnings.

—*New York Times*, July 24, 2002

When there's a problem, I have this formula. It's get it right, get it fast, get it out, get it over.

—CNN Business, November 11, 2016

DIRTY CORPORATE LAUNDRY

IT'S THE RINSE cycle where you find out how dirty the laundry has been. We're in the rinse cycle of Corporate America, and we're finding out that there was more dirty laundry than we care to admit.

—*Georgia Tech Alumni Magazine*, Winter 2003

ACCOUNTING FOR STOCK OPTIONS

WHATEVER THE MERITS of options may be, their accounting treatment is outrageous. Think for a moment of that $190 million we are going to spend for advertising at GEICO this year. Suppose that instead of paying cash for our ads, we paid the media in 10-year, at-the-market Berkshire options. Would anyone then care to argue that Berkshire had not borne a cost for advertising, or should not be charged this cost on its books?

—letter to Berkshire Hathaway shareholders, March 1999

CEO ETHICS

MOST CEOS, IT should be noted, are men and women you would be happy to have as trustees for your children's assets or as next-door neighbors. Too many of these people, however, have in recent years behaved badly at the office, fudging numbers and drawing obscene pay for mediocre business achievements. These otherwise decent people simply followed the career path of Mae West: "I was Snow White but I drifted."

—letter to Berkshire Hathaway shareholders, February 2003

Part II

WEALTH

Personal Wealth

I have every possession I want. I have a lot of friends who have a lot more possessions. But in some cases, I feel the possession possess them, rather than the other way around.

—*CBS News*, February 8, 2012

I like to be inventive. I want to be able to do what I want to do every day. And money lets you do that.

—*CBS News*, January 20, 2013

MONEY'S MAGNIFYING POWER

WHAT MONEY DOES is magnify you. Whatever kind of person you are going in—and age does this too as people get older—it magnifies both ... good and bad tendencies. Money gives you a chance if you're a slob to be a big slob—a huge slob. On the other hand, if you're inclined toward doing good things, it gives you the power to do a great many great things.

—*Georgia Tech Alumni Magazine*, Winter 2003

WEALTH AND SATISFACTION

As PEOPLE GET wealthy here, they start casting their eyes about, and they don't get more satisfied. Sometimes they get more dissatisfied. That's happened in the United States. Right now we have six times the GDP per capita, in real terms, as when I was born. Now, I don't know whether people are happier now or more discontent or what than they were in 1930. But people have a way of adjusting very quickly to things becoming better, and then any little tiny adjustment downward they can get quite unhappy about.

—CNBC, November 14, 2011

My wealth has come from a combination of living in America, some lucky genes, and compound interest.

—The Giving Pledge

THE SOURCE OF BUFFETT'S WEALTH

WHEN WE GOT married in 1952, I told Susie I was going to be rich. That wasn't going to be because of any special virtues of mine or even because of hard work, but simply because I was born with the right skills in the right place at the right time.

—*Fortune*, June 25, 2006

INHERITANCE

IF A KID comes out of the right womb in this country, they have got food stamps for their rest of their life. They just call them stocks and bonds. And their welfare officer is their trust officer.

—*PBS NewsHour*, June 27, 2017

A very rich person should leave his kids enough to do anything but not enough to do nothing.

—*Fortune*, June 25, 2006

NEITHER SUSIE NOR I ever thought we should pass huge amounts of money along to our children. Our kids are great. But I would argue that when your kids have all the advantages anyway, in terms of how they grow up and the opportunities they have for education, including what they learn at home—I would say it's neither right nor rational to be flooding them with money.

In effect, they've had a gigantic head start in a society that aspires to be a meritocracy. Dynastic megawealth would further tilt the playing field that we ought to be trying instead to level.

—*Fortune*, June 25, 2006

WEALTH IS JUST a bunch of claim checks on the activities of others in the future. You can use that wealth in any way you want to. You can cash it in or give it away. But the idea of passing wealth from generation to generation so that hundreds of your descendants can command the resources of other people simply because they came from the right womb flies in the face of a meritocratic society.

—*The Snowball*, 2008

BUFFETT'S GOOD FORTUNE

IF ALL OF us were stranded on a desert island we all landed there and we were never going to be able to get off of it—the most valuable person would be the one who could raise the most rice over time. And I could say, "Well, I can allocate capital"—you wouldn't get very excited about that.

—University of Florida, October 15, 1998

BUFFETT'S GOOD FORTUNE

I WAS BORN at the right time and place, where
the ability to allocate capital really counts. I'm
adapted to this society. I won the ovarian lottery.
I got the ball that said, "Capital Allocator—
United States."

—*BusinessWeek*, July 5, 1999

I HAVE BEEN lucky to have been born where I
was ... lucky with parents, lucky with all kinds
of things, and lucky to be wired in a way that a
market economy pays off like crazy for someone
like me. It doesn't pay off for someone who is
absolutely as good a citizen as I am—you know,
leading Boy Scout troops, teaching Sunday
school ... raising fine families—but just doesn't
happen to be wired in the same way I am.

—University of Florida, October 15, 1998

Taxes

The aggregate output of this country per capita is going to keep going up. Now who gets it depends on what government decides in terms of tax laws and all that. But America will be a wealthier country per capita five years from now, ten years from now, and twenty years from now.

—*Fortune*, December 5, 2016

WEALTHY PEOPLE'S TAX RATES

I'LL BET A million dollars against any member of the Forbes 400 who challenges me that the average [tax rate] for the Forbes 400 will be less than the average of their receptionists. I'll give 'em an 800 number. They can call me. And the million will go to whichever charity the winner designates.

—*NBC Nightly News*, October 30, 2007

FORTY PERCENT OF the revenue in the United States comes from payroll taxes, forty percent. My cleaning lady is being charged a payroll tax. Her payroll tax, counting the portion her employer pays, is higher than my capital gains tax. . . . I mean, I am treated like I am the bald eagle or something—that I have to be protected at all costs.

—CNBC, July 7, 2011

INCOME INEQUALITY

IF YOU LOOK at these 400 top incomes that have
gone from $40 million on average per family
up to $200 million, their tax rate has gone from
29 and a fraction down to 21 percent. So there's
been class warfare going on, it's just that my class
is winning. In fact my class isn't just winning,
we're killing them. It's been a rout!

—*Charlie Rose*, September 30, 2011

THIS SYSTEM WORKS for the people involved. It
works for the wealthy, it works for the special
interests, it works for people in Congress and it
works for the lobbyists. And it may not work for
my cleaning lady, but, you know, what can she do
about it?

—CNBC, November 14, 2011

If there's a class war, you know, we're the ones that are waging it, the rich. And our soldiers are the lobbyists. And the poor have a bunch of little toy soldiers.

—CNBC, November 14, 2011

ON THE 2017 BETTER CARE RECONCILIATION ACT

IF THE [SENATE Republicans' Better Care Reconciliation Act] bill . . . had been in effect this year . . . I would have saved $679,999, or over 17 percent of my tax bill.

There's nothing ambiguous about that. I will be given a 17 percent tax cut. And the people it's directed at are couples with $250,000 or more of income. You could entitle this, you know, Relief for the Rich Act or something, because . . . I have got friends where it would have saved them as much as—it gets into the $10-million-and-up figure.

—*PBS NewsHour*, June 27, 2017

I THINK MEMBERS of the Senate and the House get $174,000 a year. But . . . if you look at the disclosures, they have substantial other income. If they get to higher than $250,000, as a married couple, or $200,000 as a single person, they have given themselves a big, big tax cut, if they voted for this.

—*PBS NewsHour*, June 27, 2017

TAX RETURNS

I HAVE PAID federal income tax every year since 1944, when I was 13. (Though, being a slow starter, I owed only $7 in tax that year.) I have copies of all 72 of my returns and none uses a carryforward.

Finally, I have been audited by the IRS multiple times and am currently being audited. I have no problem in releasing my tax information while under audit. Neither would Mr. Trump—at least he would have no *legal* problem.

—**press release, October 10, 2016**

[Hedge fund operators] say they work hard, and in the process of working hard, they make other people money. And that's true of a whole bunch of people in the world, but that doesn't entitle them to a preferential tax rate.

—*NBC Nightly News*, October 30, 2007

SHARED SACRIFICE

OUR LEADERS HAVE asked for "shared sacrifice." But when they did the asking, they spared me. I checked with my megarich friends to learn what pain they were expecting. They, too, were left untouched. While the poor and middle class fight for us in Afghanistan, and while most Americans struggle to make ends meet, we megarich continue to get our extraordinary tax breaks.

—*New York Times,* August 14, 2011

THE ESTATE TAX

IF YOU ELIMINATE the $20 billion or so raised by the estate tax, you've got to make the money up by taxing everybody else somehow. It's amazing how the American population will fight for the families of those few thousand people who pay large estate taxes and for the whole rest of the country to pay for it out of their pockets.

—*The Snowball,* 2008

BERKSHIRE'S TAX BILL

WRITING CHECKS TO the IRS that include strings of zeros does not bother Charlie or me. Berkshire as a corporation, and we as individuals, have prospered in America as we would have in no other country. Indeed, if we lived in some other part of the world and completely escaped taxes, I'm sure we would be worse off financially (and in many other ways as well). Overall, we feel extraordinarily lucky to have been dealt a hand in life that enables us to write large checks to the government rather than one requiring the government to regularly write checks to us—say, because we are disabled or unemployed.

—letter to Berkshire Hathaway shareholders,
March 1999

TAXES WON'T CHANGE ENTREPRENEURIAL SPIRIT

LET'S FORGET ABOUT the rich and ultrarich going on strike and stuffing their ample funds under their mattresses if—gasp—capital gains rates and ordinary income rates are increased. The ultrarich, including me, will forever pursue investment opportunities.

—*New York Times*, November 25, 2012

A HISTORY OF CORPORATE TAXATION

ANYBODY THAT THINKS our corporate taxes are too high should look at a chart of corporate taxes as a percentage of GDP since World War II, and it's come down from 4 percent of GDP to 2 percent of GDP, while many other forms of taxes have, obviously, increased. And American business earnings on net tangible assets, which is the way to measure profitability overall, you know, it's basically the envy of the world. . . .

And our tax rates now for corporations are far lower than when Charlie and I were operating. And American business actually was doing pretty good then.

—Berkshire Hathaway annual meeting, May 3, 2014

REVENUE-NEUTRAL TAX REFORM

YOU CAN TAKE the rate down and make it revenue neutral by knocking out all those special things. I have nothing against that. That would benefit Berkshire, frankly, but I will tell you, if it's going to be revenue neutral, it means just as many people are going to have their taxes increased as decreased, and the ones that are going to have them increased are going to be flooding the Capitol with lobbyists. If it's going to be revenue neutral, that means billions and billions and billions more are going to come from some companies, because we're going to pay less at Berkshire.

—CNBC, November 14, 2011

LOBBYING AND THE TAX CODE

EVERY LINE IN the tax code is there because someone was fighting for it. The people who care about that line are concentrated and focused on it, and people who are affected by that line are diffused and really not even aware of it.

—*Haaretz*, March 23, 2011

THE TAX LAW has been shaped not by logic, but by K Street.

—CNBC, July 7, 2011

THE "BUFFETT RULE"

IN THE LAST 25 years, the Forbes 400 list has had its net worth increase nine for one.... That is not happening with the American people generally, and it's happening during a time when those same rich people have had their tax rates go down, down, down. And I think that when we're talking to 312 million Americans about shared sacrifice and taking away things we promised to them ... it's time for the ultrarich to share in that sacrifice to some degree....

I mean, you change the Social Security rule somewhat and millions of people will feel it, they'll really feel it. You change the Medicare rules and millions of people will feel it. You get a minimum tax of 30 or 35 percent on incomes of a million or 10 million or over, the truth is, those people won't even feel it. But at least the American people, as a whole, will feel somehow that the ultrarich have been asked to participate to a small degree in this overall sacrifice that we're all going to be asked to participate in.

—CNBC, November 14, 2011

IT'S VERY IMPORTANT in terms of getting people to make the kind of sacrifices they're going to face. We're going to be telling people that some of the promises are going to have to be modified, and these are people that don't have a lot of margin of safety in their own affairs. They're not like me, they can't just sell a few stocks or something like that if the payment doesn't come through or this or that.

The ultrarich who are paying really subnormal taxes—and there's a lot of them that aren't, but there are a lot of them that are—I think it's a terrible mistake to ask 300 million Americans to tighten their belts and ignore that group.

—*Charlie Rose*, September 30, 2011

I'D RATHER HAVE some home run that was hit in Yankee Stadium named after me. You know, "That was the Buffett Home Run" or something of the sort.

—CNBC, November 14, 2011

EARNED INCOME TAX CREDIT

THE BETTER ANSWER [to income inequality]
is a major and carefully crafted expansion of
the Earned Income Tax Credit (EITC), which
currently goes to millions of low-income
workers. Payments to eligible workers diminish
as their earnings increase. But there is no
disincentive effect: A gain in wages always
produces a gain in overall income. The process is
simple: You file a tax return, and the government
sends you a check.

—*Wall Street Journal*, May 21, 2015

AN EARNED INCOME Tax Credit, I think, is the
best way of both guaranteeing that people have a
reasonable amount in their pocket even if they're
working at jobs where the market ... wouldn't
pay that much. And it also keeps the dignity of
work there. And it also encourages people to
improve their skills because as you move up, you
keep more of the money.

—CNBC, February 26, 2018

Philanthropy

GIVING BACK TO SOCIETY

ANDREW CARNEGIE . . . said that huge fortunes that flow in large part from society should in large part be returned to society. In my case, the ability to allocate capital would have had little utility unless I lived in a rich, populous country in which enormous quantities of marketable securities were traded and were sometimes ridiculously mispriced. And fortunately for me, that describes the United States in the second half of the last century.

—*Fortune*, June 25, 2006

TOUGH PROBLEMS

IN PHILANTHROPY YOU'RE tackling the very
tough problems that have resisted intellect and
money in the past. In business you're looking for
something easy to do, maybe just a new improved
product that will sell a little bit better than the
previous one. So in philanthropy, if you're doing
important things, you have to expect mistakes.

—NPR, October 28, 2013

NO MARKET FEEDBACK

YOU DO NOT have a market system feedback.
You set up a hamburger stand and you are
turning out lousy hamburgers, you will know it
by the end of the day. In philanthropy, if you are
doing something dumb, you will have people
encouraging you to do more of the dumb thing. So,
it has no market feedback, and that's a huge issue

—*Haaretz*, March 23, 2011

GIVING WHAT YOU HAVE

I HAVE THE much greater admiration, frankly, for the person who drops $5 or $1 in the collection plate on Sunday where it makes a difference in whether they go take their kids to a movie or whether they go to eat out or something of that sort. They are actually giving up something that has utility to them. I am giving up nothing that has utility to me. I have everything in the world I want that can be bought by money.

—Georgetown University, September 19, 2013

My instincts are to
go along the idea of
encouraging individual
philanthropy. But
I do not believe in
giving away other
people's money, and so
Berkshire Hathaway,
at the parent-
company level, does
not make charitable
contributions.

—Forbes 400 Summit on Philanthropy, June 26, 2012

TEN-YEAR HORIZON

WHEN I DIE, all of the money has to be spent within 10 years after the estate has closed, because I do not think that I can pick out some little great-great-grandchild yet to be born, you know, just because he has the right name of Buffett or she has the right name, and they will be the best custodians. I mean, there will be plenty of philanthropists 50 years after I die to take care of the problems of 50 years, but I want the money to get spent promptly and I don't believe in trying to control things from the grave. I mean, I like to think I can think outside the box, but thinking outside of that particular box?

—Georgetown University, September 19, 2013

GIVING TO THE GATES FOUNDATION

I CAME TO realize that there was a terrific foundation that was already scaled up—that wouldn't have to go through the real grind of getting to a megasize like the Buffett Foundation would—and that could productively use my money now....

Over the years I had gotten to know Bill and Melinda Gates well, spent a lot of time with them having fun, and way beyond that, had grown to admire what they were doing with their foundation. I've seen them give presentations about its programs, and I'm always amazed at the enthusiasm and passion and energy they're pouring into their work. They've gone at it, you might say, with both head and heart.

Fortune, June 25, 2006

GIVING TO THE GATES FOUNDATION

HE HAS THIS view that every human life worldwide is the equivalent of every other human life, and he's backing it up not only with money, but backing it up with his time. And his wife, Melinda, is backing it up with her time. And they are really going to spend, you know, the last half of their lives or so using . . . money, talent, energy, imagination, all improving the lives of 6.5 billion people around the world. That's what I admire the most.

—Columbia University, November 12, 2009

GIVING TO THE GATES FOUNDATION

I'M GETTING TWO people enormously successful
at something, where I've had a chance to see
what they've done, where I know they will keep
doing it—where they've done it with their own
money, so they're not living in some fantasy
world—and where in general I agree with their
reasoning. If I've found the right vehicle for my
goal, there's no reason to wait.

Compare what I'm doing with them to my
situation at Berkshire, where I have talented and
proven people in charge of our businesses. They
do a much better job than I could in running
their operations. What can be more logical, in
whatever you want done, than finding someone
better equipped than you are to do it? Who
wouldn't select Tiger Woods to take his place in a
high-stakes golf game?

—*Fortune,* June 25, 2006

Part III

WIT AND WISDOM

Politics and Current Events

PERSONAL POLITICS

I HAVE NOT put my politics in a blind trust. On the other hand, I don't speak for Berkshire in doing that. Berkshire, to my knowledge, Berkshire the parent company never had any contributions to politicians. And I don't believe [in] imposing my views on 370,000 employees and a million shareholders. I mean, I'm not their nanny on that.

— CNBC, February 26, 2018

BETTING ON THE UNITED STATES

IT'S ALWAYS BEEN a mistake to bet against America, since 1776. And, you know, we take our body blows from time to time, but this country always comes through. And when we get united, get out of the way.... And of course, after 9/11 we saw it. But I've always had enormous faith in this country to do anything, whether it's in economics or whether it's in liberating people or whatever it may be.

—CNBC, May 2, 2011

ECONOMIC RECOVERY

I THINK THE big factor in the continuation of the recovery will be the Steve Jobses of the world coming up with new products that nobody thought of before. And millions of Americans doing what people before them have done, trying to think of ways to do them more efficiently.... Capitalism works, and I think we're seeing it work.

—CNBC, May 2, 2011

GEICO GOT IN trouble in the mid '70s. American Express got in trouble in the mid '60s. Those are two of the greatest investments I've ever had, and you had to look out five or ten years out. That's what you have to do with the economy, incidentally. We have a wonderful economy in the United States over time, and it will come back, just like GEICO came back and American Express came back.

—*Charlie Rose*, September 30, 2011

NOTHING RIVALS THE market system in producing what people want—nor, even more so, in delivering what people don't yet know they want. My parents, when young, could not envision a television set, nor did I, in my 50s, think I needed a personal computer. Both products, once people saw what they could do, quickly revolutionized their lives. I now spend ten hours a week playing bridge online. And, as I write this letter, "search" is invaluable to me. (I'm not ready for Tinder, however.)

—letter to Berkshire Hathaway shareholders,
February 2016

THE UNITED STATES SINCE 1930

I WAS BORN in August of 1930. You know, if a genie had come to me and said, "Warren, in the next two years, the Dow is going to go from 180 down to 40, there's going to be 4,000 banks closed. You know, there's going to be a dust bowl in Nebraska where you live, and farm prices are going to go to hell, and in another 10 years we're going to have a surprise attack by an enemy that looks like it's going to win the war for a while, we're going to have nuclear bombs"—you know, I'm not sure I would have come out. . . . But the truth was that America, in the 80 years since I've been born, the average person lives six times better than when I was born.

—CNBC, July 7, 2011

THE UNITED STATES SINCE 1930

I'M 80 YEARS old, and in the 80 years since then, the average standard of living for Americans has improved six for one in real terms. Six for one! You go back to the Middle Ages, you went centuries and you were lucky if you were looking at a 1 percent increase. When I came out of the womb in 1930, we faced a depression, we faced a world war that it looked like we were losing, but the system works. It unleashes human potential.

—*Haaretz*, March 23, 2011

THE UNITED STATES SOLVES PROBLEMS

IF YOU LOOK back on the 19th century, we had seven great bank panics. If you look back at the 20th century, we had the Great Depression and world wars and flu epidemics. This country doesn't avoid problems. It just solves them.

—Columbia University, November 12, 2009

I do think it's very important that business be a handmaiden of government. Business has done wonderful things for America, and America has done wonderful things for business.

—CNBC, June 7, 2018

I think that's a podium that we should have. We will be the economic leader, and we should be the moral leader. We should stand for more than the fact that we're the wealthiest country.

—*PBS NewsHour*, June 26, 2017

AMERICA IS ALREADY GREAT

ALL MY LIFE I've heard people talk about how
terrible things are. You know, you're hearing it
in the political campaign now. You know, "Make
America great again." America's great now, it's
never been greater. It's ridiculous.

—Fortune Most Powerful Women Summit,
October 13, 2015

A ONE-PERSON SOLUTION?

[DONALD TRUMP] SAYS, "No one knows the
system better than me, which is why I alone can
fix it." Well la-di-da, you know! I mean, this is—
only he can fix it! I didn't really realize we were
in such grave danger. I mean, there's 325 million
Americans, and if this guy leaves for Canada, it's
supposed to be hopeless for the rest of us.

—Hillary Clinton rally in Omaha, Nebraska,
August 1, 2016

GIVE A MONKEY A DART

[TRUMP HOTELS AND Casino Resorts] loses money every year, every single year. [Trump] takes out $44 million in compensation during that period. In 1995, when he offered this company, if a monkey had thrown a dart at the stock page, the monkey on average would have made 150 percent. But the people that believed in ['Trump], that listened to his siren song, came away losing well over 90 cents on the dollar. They got back less than a dime.

—Hillary Clinton rally in Omaha, Nebraska,
August 1, 2016

THE BANKRUPTCY BRAGGART

I'VE REALLY NEVER known another businessman that brags about his bankruptcies, you know. I mean, and to tell you the truth, why not? I mean, it's his claim to stardom. I don't know anybody else that's had six bankruptcies.

—Hillary Clinton rally in Omaha, Nebraska,
August 1, 2016

I don't read economic forecasts. I don't read the funny papers.

—*BusinessWeek*, July 5, 1999

WE HAVE NEVER either bought a business or not bought a business because of any macro feeling of any kind. We don't read predictions about interest rates or business or anything like that because it doesn't make any difference. I mean let's say in 1972 when we bought See's Candy—I think maybe Nixon put on the price controls a little bit later. Let's say we'd seen that, but so what? We'd have missed the chance to buy something for $25 million that's earning $60 million pre-tax now. We don't want to pass up the chance to do something intelligent because of some prediction about something that we're no good on anyway.

—University of Florida, October 15, 1998

DIVIDING THE ECONOMIC PIE

EVEN IN A rich family they may argue about who gets most of the income, and I am sure they do. We have a very rich family in the United States. The old would want more, the young would want more, the people who are in their productive years would like to give less to those who aren't. The pie will never be big enough to take care of everyone's desires.

—*Haaretz*, March 23, 2011

We were promised that a rising tide would lift all boats. A rising tide has lifted all yachts.

—*CBS News*, February 8, 2012

OBJECTIVES OF ECONOMIC POLICY

IN MY MIND, the country's economic policies should have two main objectives. First, we should wish, in our rich society, for every person who is willing to work to receive income that will provide him or her a decent lifestyle. Second, any plan to do that should not distort our market system, the key element required for growth and prosperity.

—*Wall Street Journal,* May 21, 2015

GLOBAL TRADE

THERE WILL BE an element in the United States or in other countries that resists the idea of more trade between countries. I am in exactly the opposite camp and believe that we will prosper as we do more and more business with each other. Various countries have various advantages and no country can do all things themselves. As world trade expands it will mean a better life for people around the world.

—*Forbes India,* April 20, 2011

THE BENEFITS OF free trade are diffused over 320 million people. You buy your shoes a little cheaper; you buy your underwear a little cheaper, because of free trade. But the penalties to the person involved, the steel worker in Ohio or the textile worker in Massachusetts are very, very extreme.... I think that we need to have free trade and we have to have policies that moderate and hopefully even cure the damage that are done to the lives of people who are perfectly decent citizens, who've spent their life in one trade and at 55, they're not going to be able to retrain for something else very well.

—*Fortune*, December 5, 2016

INFLATION

INFLATION, SOMEONE SAID many years ago, is an invisible tax that only one man in a million really understands. It is a tax on people that have had faith in their currency, the governments issued it. The best investment against inflation is to improve your own earning power, your own talent. Very few people maximize their talent. If you increase your talent, they can't tax it or they can't take it away from you.

—*Forbes India*, April 20, 2011

EVERY TIME I get worried about inflation I think about how 94 percent of that dollar bill from when I was born isn't worth anything, yet I seem to have done pretty well, so it can't destroy everything.

—*Haaretz*, March 23, 2011

CREATING JOBS

I'M VERY SUSPICIOUS when people say, you know, "This will create jobs," and "If I open a hamburger stand, it'll create jobs." There's a lot of rhetoric that gets a little loose. If you're really seriously hurting the environment [to create 20,000 jobs], you can have those 20,000 people start building me a tomb.

—CNBC, November 14, 2011

THE 2008 FINANCIAL CRISIS

PEOPLE WERE WATCHING a movie and they thought the movie had a happy ending and all of a sudden the events on the screen started telling them something different. And different people in the audience picked it up maybe [at] different hours, different days, different weeks. But at some point the bubble popped.

—remarks to the Financial Crisis Inquiry Commission,
May 26, 2010

THE 2008 FINANCIAL CRISIS

THE AMERICAN PEOPLE, including banks, Congress, the administration, Freddie Mac and Fannie Mae, the media—they all subscribed to the idea that residential housing could not collapse.... It was a collective delusion, that once adopted, spread through all kinds of institutions and instruments of finance so that the interdependence of these items, once the delusion became exposed, once it became apparent that the emperor had no clothes, swept through the economy with the impact and the speed of a tsunami.

—*Haaretz*, March 23, 2011

WHEN IT REALLY became apparent that, you know, that this was something like we'd never seen was in September 2008. That's when I said on CNBC, "This is an economic Pearl Harbor." ... I meant that I hadn't seen it three months earlier because I didn't see a Pearl Harbor three months earlier.

—remarks to the Financial Crisis Inquiry Commission, May 26, 2010

GOVERNMENT INTERVENTION IN THE
FINANCIAL CRISIS

WHATEVER THE DOWNSIDES may be, strong
and immediate action by government was
essential last year if the financial system was
to avoid a total breakdown. Had one occurred,
the consequences for every area of our economy
would have been cataclysmic. Like it or not, the
inhabitants of Wall Street, Main Street, and the
various Side Streets of America were all in the
same boat.

—letter to Berkshire Hathaway shareholders,
February 2009

ONLY THE GOVERNMENT could have saved things.
The whole world wanted to deleverage. And they
were deleveraging under conditions of extreme
haste und with guns to their head in some cases.
And the only entity that could possibly leverage
up at the same time that everybody else wanted
to deleverage was the federal government.

—Columbia University, November 12, 2009

WE SHOULD THANK Bernanke and Paulson and President Bush and President Obama and Tim Geithner for doing a lot of things that helped us get out of what could've been a terrible, terrible mess. It was a mess. But we really were right at the abyss and we had—we had a government that did the right things. Maybe they did some wrong things earlier, maybe they didn't do it perfectly. But I give them great credit and this country's best days lie ahead, believe me.

—CNBC, November 14, 2011

If [Bank of America CEO] Ken Lewis hadn't have bought Merrill on Sunday, I think the system would have stopped, you know. He is the guy that turned out to have saved the system.

—remarks to the Financial Crisis Inquiry Commission, May 26, 2010

OPPORTUNITIES DURING THE FINANCIAL CRISIS

I DON'T LIKE to sound, you know, like a mortician during an epidemic or anything, but last fall [of 2008] was really quite exciting for me. I don't wish it on anybody, but there were things being offered. There are opportunities for us to do things that didn't exist a year or two earlier.

—Columbia University, November 12, 2009

FRAUD IN THE FINANCIAL SYSTEM

THERE WAS FRAUD on the parts of the borrowers and there were frauds on part of the intermediaries in some cases. But you better not have a system that is dependent on the absence of fraud. It will be with us.

—remarks to the Financial Crisis Inquiry Commission, May 26, 2010

Credit is like oxygen. When either is abundant, its presence goes unnoticed. When either is missing, that's *all* that is noticed. Even a short absence of credit can bring a company to its knees.

—letter to Berkshire Hathaway shareholders, February 2011

We were in the bar drinking. I'm not sure that we want to go all the way back in, but we ought to get over the hangover.

—*Charlie Rose*, September 30, 2011

Well, there'll be [another financial crisis] sometime, but no, I don't worry about it in the least ... because I conduct myself so that if there's another crisis I'll still be around, Berkshire will be in good shape.

—CNBC, September 12, 2018

THE US BUDGET AND TRADE DEFICITS

WE WILL NOT be spending 25 percent of GDP and raising 15 percent of GDP 10 years from now. We'll get there somehow. But ... everybody in the country is trying to figure out how to have somebody else pay for it. But some of them are better equipped to fight that fight than others and they're the people with money that care and that hire lobbyists.

—CNBC, November 14, 2011

RAISING THE DEBT CEILING

WE RAISED THE debt ceiling seven times during the Bush administration and now in this administration, they're using it as a hostage. You really don't have any business playing Russian roulette to get your way in some other matter. We should be more grown up than that.

—CNBC, July 7, 2011

THE SIMPSON-BOWLES PLAN

I THINK WHAT happened with Simpson-Bowles
was an absolute tragedy. I mean, here are
two extremely high-grade people, they have
somewhat different ideas about government.
But they're smart, they're decent, they've got
good senses of humor, too. They're good at
working with people. They work like the devil
for 10 months or something like that. They
compromise, they bring in people as far apart
as Durbin and Coburn to get them to sign on,
and then they're totally ignored. I think that's a
travesty.

—CNBC, November 14, 2011

GOVERNMENT DEBT

THE IMPORTANT THING on government debt is
how much is owed externally. ... The national
debt is largely held internally, but the game
is changing as we run a trade deficit. So the
trade deficit is a threat, essentially, to living as
well as we live now. We are, essentially, selling
off a little piece of the farm every day, as we
run a trade deficit in order to finance our own
consumption. We've got a very big rich farm, so
we can sell a little piece of that farm for a long
time without hardly noticing it. ... We are giving
the rest of the world claim checks on us. That has
consequences over time.

—**University of Notre Dame, spring 1991**

FUNDING PROMISES

LOCAL AND STATE financial problems are accelerating, in large part because public entities promised pensions they couldn't afford. Citizens and public officials typically under-appreciated the gigantic financial tapeworm that was born when promises were made that conflicted with a willingness to fund them.

—letter to Berkshire Hathaway shareholders,
February 2014

DEMOCRACY IN THE UNITED STATES

WE ARE STILL a democracy, but we have moved in my lifetime toward a plutocracy. We do not have a plutocracy, I want to emphasize that, but the distribution of wealth and the influence of wealth have moved in that direction.

—*Haaretz*, March 23, 2011

ON WOMEN

THE MOMENT I emerged from my mother's womb . . . my possibilities dwarfed those of my siblings, for I was a boy! And my brainy, personable, and good-looking siblings were not. My parents would love us equally, and our teachers would give us similar grades. But at every turn my sisters would be told—more through signals than words—that success for them would be "marrying well." I was meanwhile hearing that the world's opportunities were there for me to seize.

So my floor became my sisters' ceiling—and nobody thought much about ripping up that pattern until a few decades ago. Now, thank heavens, the structural barriers for women are falling.

—*Fortune*, May 2, 2013

ON WOMEN

I'M HAPPY TO say that funhouse mirrors are becoming less common among the women I meet. Try putting one in front of my daughter. She'll just laugh and smash it. Women should never forget that it is common for powerful and seemingly self-assured males to have more than a bit of the Wizard of Oz in them. Pull the curtain aside, and you'll often discover they are not supermen after all.

—*Fortune,* May 2, 2013

THE DEATH OF OSAMA BIN LADEN

A MASS MURDERER of almost incomprehensible dimensions has been eliminated, just as was the case with Hitler. But there are lots of people in the world that are going to have evil intent toward this country ... as well as other people, and they're not going to go away. And they're going to continue to seek ways to hurt us, disrupt us, and I think our government has done really quite an amazing job.

—CNBC, May 2, 2011

SEPTEMBER 11, 2001

I REALLY THOUGHT we were going to get hit again. And the reason we haven't been hit again, you know, we won't know all the reasons. But somebody has done a lot of things right ... over the years, both administrations, to keep that from happening. But the desire to do us harm exists in the hearts of too many people around the world, and they're looking for new ways to do it, and we need an ever-vigilant government, and I think we have one.

—CNBC, May 2, 2011

WHY, YOU MIGHT ask, didn't I recognize the [risk of terrorist attacks] *before* September 11th? The answer, sadly, is that I did—but I didn't convert thought into action. I violated the Noah rule: Predicting rain doesn't count; building arks does.

—letter to Berkshire Hathaway shareholders,
February 2002

CHINA AND THE United States, over time, will largely get along. We largely have the same interests. We both have nuclear bombs, so it's not in our interest to start getting really furious with each other. And there will be tensions. We'll want to play the game our way, and they'll want to play the game their way, and we'll both have to give in some cases.

—CNBC, November 14, 2011

THEY ARE STARTING to unleash human potential in China the same way we've been unleashing human potential since 1776. And I'm all for that. We should much prefer to have a prosperous China than a China that has problems. If you postulate two worlds, one in which we're an island of prosperity, 315 million, and the rest of the world is sitting there envious, or postulate something where the rest of the world is growing even faster than we are, but we're also benefiting, just choose which world you want.

—Fortune Most Powerful Women Summit,
October 16, 2013

POWER OF IMMIGRANTS

WE MAY BE sitting here because two Jewish immigrants signed a letter to Roosevelt after fleeing Europe and coming to the United States. Einstein and Leo Szilard wrote the president and warned him that Nazi Germany was developing nuclear weapons. . . . The quality of immigrants, the motivation of immigrants, this is what has contributed to the greatness of the country.

—The *Atlantic*, February 26, 2017

THE EURO CRISIS

THEY HAVE TRIED an experiment where the imperfections in it are becoming manifest. . . . They melded into a single currency for 17 countries, but they didn't meld the culture, they didn't meld the fiscal policies. They either have to come closer together in a major way, or they need to separate.

—*Charlie Rose*, September 30, 2011

BARACK OBAMA

LOOKING BACK, HE probably should have prepared the American public somewhat better for what laid ahead.... There was not going to be some magic wand when he came in 2009. I admire him enormously and the actions taken, but to the extent that people thought we were going to cure everything in six months or eight months or ten months, that was a mistake.

—*Charlie Rose*, September 30, 2011

BARACK OBAMA'S LEGACY

I THINK WE will talk about a president [who], where our economic machine came off the tracks like it hadn't since the 1930s, put it back on the tracks and got it going very well. And I think that's huge.

—CNN Business, November 11, 2016

ENVIRONMENTAL DISASTER

PASCAL, IT MAY be recalled, argued that if there were only a tiny probability that God truly existed, it made sense to behave as if He did because the rewards could be infinite whereas the lack of belief risked eternal misery. Likewise, if there is only a 1% chance the planet is heading toward a truly major disaster and delay means passing a point of no return, inaction now is foolhardy. Call this Noah's Law: If an ark may be essential for *survival*, begin building it today, no matter how cloudless the skies appear.

—letter to Berkshire Hathaway shareholders, February 2016

GUN MANUFACTURERS

WE DON'T OWN any gun manufacturers but I have not issued any edict, for example, to the two managers that run money besides me at Berkshire that they can't own stock in gun manufacturers.

—CNBC, February 26, 2018

WEAPONS OF MASS DESTRUCTION

I THINK THE number-one problem of mankind is weapons of mass destruction. I mean, we have learned since 1945 how somebody with bad intent or some organization with bad intent or occasionally, some government with bad intent, the knowledge is there of how to kill millions of people. And in some cases, the intent might be there.

—CNBC, May 7, 2018

Life Lessons

The biggest lesson
I got is the power of
unconditional love. If
you offer that to your
child you're 90 percent
of the way home. If
every parent out there
can extend that to their
child at a very young
age– it's going to make
for a better human
being.

—*The Huffington Post*, July 8, 2010

BUFFETT'S FATHER

MY DAD . . . he was really a maverick. But
he wasn't a maverick for the sake of being a
maverick. He just didn't care what other people
thought. My dad taught me how life should be
lived.

—*The Snowball*, 2008

I NEVER SAW my dad do anything in his entire
life that [he] wouldn't feel good about being
on the front page of the paper. . . . He gave me
unconditional love. . . . He was a terrific human
being.

—*CBS News*, February 8, 2012

BUFFETT'S ADVANTAGES

WHEN I WAS a kid, I got all kinds of good things. I had the advantage of a home where people talked about interesting things, and I had intelligent parents and I went to decent schools. I don't think I could have been raised with a better pair of parents. That was enormously important. I didn't get money from my parents, and I really didn't want it. But I was born at the right time and place.

—The Snowball, 2008

CHILDHOOD REBELLION

I WAS REALLY rebelling [as a child]. Some of the teachers predicted that I was going to be a disastrous failure. I set the record for checks on deficiencies in deportment and all that. But my dad never gave up on me. And my mother didn't either, actually. Neither one. It's great to have parents that believe in you.

—The Snowball, 2008

THE FREEDOM TO CHOOSE

MY OWN DAD had given me a terrific gift: he told me, both verbally and by his behavior, that he cared only about the values I had, not the particular path I chose. He simply said that he had unlimited confidence in me and that I should follow my dreams. I was thereby freed of all expectations except to do my best.

—foreword, *40 Chances: Finding Hope in a Hungry World,* 2013

LEARNING ETHICS

I THINK THE best place to learn ethics is in the home. I think most of us get our values from what we see around us before we get to business school. I think that it's important to emphasize them, but I think that if I had a choice of having great education and ethics fully on in the home or as a course in a school later on, I would choose the home.

—Columbia University, November 12, 2009

SUSIE WAS AS big an influence on me as my
dad, or bigger probably, in a different way. I had
all these defense mechanisms that she could
explain, but I can't. She probably saw things in
me that other people couldn't see. But she knew
it would take time and a lot of nourishment
to bring it out. She made me feel that I had
somebody with a little sprinkling can who was
going to make sure that the flowers grew.

—*The Snowball*, 2008

Marry the right person. And I'm serious about that. It will make more difference in your life. It will change your aspiration, all kind of things. It's enormously important who you marry.

—Columbia University, November 12, 2009

CHOOSE PEOPLE WHO ARE BETTER THAN YOU

IT'S VERY IMPORTANT in life to associate with people that are better than you are. And it's the most important decision—you will go in the direction of the people that you associate with. And you'll get ideas from them and you'll see how their behavior works and all of that sort of thing.

—CNBC, May 7, 2018

SEEK DISAGREEMENT

IF YOU START selecting your investments, or your friends, or your neighbors, based on trying to get people that agree with you totally, you're going to live a pretty peculiar life, I think.

—Berkshire Hathaway annual meeting, May 5, 2019

I don't believe in making life plans.

—*Forbes*, November 1, 1969

Jay-Z HAD BEEN out here about a year ago. And what I did was I admired his tie about six times. I said, "Boy, that is a good-looking tie, Jay." And finally he said, "OK, you win, Warren." And he took it off and he gave it to me.

[Later] I went to this opening. I wore the tie he gave me. And then, when I saw him, I started looking at his tie. And I said, "You know, Jay, that is one good-looking tie." And he said, "Warren . . . forget it, you only get one."

—*CBS News*, February 8, 2012

DAILY ROUTINE

I SPEND AN inordinate amount of time reading. I probably read at least six hours a day, maybe more. And I spend an hour or two on the telephone. And I think. That's about it.

—University of Nebraska–Lincoln, October 10, 1994

PATIENCE

[CAPITAL CITIES/ABC CEO] Tom Murphy, 40 years ago, said to me one day, "You know, Warren, you can tell a guy to go to hell tomorrow. You don't give up the right. So just keep your mouth shut today, and see if you feel the same way tomorrow." That's terrific advice. I don't know how many problems that's saved me.

—*The Huffington Post*, July 8, 2010

I FEEL LIKE I'm on my back and there's the Sistine Chapel, and I'm painting away. I like it when people say, "Gee, that's a pretty good-looking painting." But it's my painting, and when somebody says, "Why don't you use more red instead of blue?" Goodbye. It's my painting. And I don't care what they sell it for. The painting itself will never be finished. That's one of the great things about it.

—*The Snowball*, 2008

I DO NOT believe in taking baby steps when you see something that you really understand. I never want to do anything on a small scale because, what's the reason? If I'm doing it on a small scale because I'm not that sure of my opinion, I'll forget it entirely and go on to something I'm sure about.

—University of Nebraska–Lincoln, October 10, 1994.

I was lucky enough to get the right foundation very early on. And then basically I didn't listen to anybody else. I just look in the mirror every morning and the mirror always agrees with me.

—Columbia University, November 12, 2009

THE INNER SCORECARD

THE BIG QUESTION about how people behave is whether they've got an Inner Scorecard or an Outer Scorecard. It helps if you can be satisfied with an Inner Scorecard. I always pose it this way. I say: "Lookit. Would you rather be the world's greatest lover, but have everyone think you're the world's worst lover? Or would you rather be the world's worst lover but have everyone think you're the world's greatest lover?"

The Snowball, 2008

Your best investment is yourself. There is nothing that compares to it.

—*Georgia Tech Alumni Magazine*, Winter 2003

YOUR BEST INVESTMENT

ADDRESS WHATEVER YOU feel your weaknesses are, and do it now. I was terrified of public speaking when I was young. I couldn't do it. It cost me $100 to take a Dale Carnegie course, and it changed my life. I got so confident about my new ability, I proposed to my wife during the middle of the course. It also helped me sell stocks in Omaha, despite being 21 and looking even younger. Nobody can take away what you've got in yourself—and everybody has potential they haven't used yet.

—*Forbes*, September 19, 2017

FINANCIAL LITERACY

NOT EVERYBODY'S GOING to be an entrepreneur, but everybody should be financially literate. Financial literacy is a base requirement like spelling or reading or something of the sort that everybody should acquire at any early age. The financial habits you develop when you are young are going to go with you into your adulthood.

—*Reuters*, May 19, 2014

If you work with people who cause your stomach to churn, I'd say get another job. That is a terrible way to go through life, and you only go through life once.

—*Georgia Tech Alumni Magazine,* Winter 2003

LOVING YOUR WORK

YOU GOTTA DO what you love. You've got to have a passion for it. If you're not doing it, get into something else. There is something out there for you. . . . As long as you are doing something that you enjoy, it doesn't really make a difference whether you've got $10 million or $100 million or $1 million. You want to have enough so you can do most of the things in life you like doing. That doesn't take a fortune.

—*Georgia Tech Alumni Magazine*, Winter 2003

DO WHAT YOU would do if you were in my position, where the money means nothing to you. At 79 . . . I work every day. And it's what I want to do more than anything else in the world. The closer you can come to that early on in your life, you know the more fun you're going to have in life and really the better you're going to do.

—Columbia University, November 12, 2009

INTEGRITY

THERE WAS A fellow that—Pete Kiewit, in Omaha—used to say that he looked for three things in hiring people. He looked for integrity, intelligence, and energy. And he said if a person didn't have the first . . . that the latter two would kill him. Because if they don't have integrity, you want 'em dumb and lazy. You don't want 'em smart and energetic.

—**University of Florida, October 15, 1998**

THINK FOR A moment that I granted you the right to buy 10 percent of one of your classmates for the rest of his or her lifetime.... Which one are you going to pick? ... Pick the one with the highest IQ? I doubt it. Are you going to pick the one with the best grades? I doubt it. You're not even going to pick the most energetic one necessarily or the one that displays initiative, but you're going to start looking for qualitative factors in addition, because everyone has enough brain power and energy.... You'd probably pick the one who you responded the best to. The one that was going to have the leadership qualities. The one that was going to be able to get other people to carry out their interests. That would be the person who was generous and honest, and who gave credit to other people even for their own ideas.

—University of Florida, October 15, 1998

By far, the most important quality is not how much IQ you've got. IQ is not the scarce factor. You need a reasonable amount of intelligence, but the *temperament* is 90 percent of it.

—University of Notre Dame, spring 1991

OLD AGE

WHEN YOU'RE 81, you're gonna have more fun than you're having now. I mean, 81 is a great year. I look forward to doing what I do.... I forget whether it was Mel Ott, when he was playing for the Giants or somebody, said, "You know, they—you mean they pay me for this?" That's the way I feel.

—*CBS News*, February 8, 2012

THE PERFECT JOB FOR AN OLD MAN

THIS JOB DOESN'T really require hand-eye coordination or stamina or anything. You know, you just sit at a desk and you apply things that you learned 60 or 70 years ago, and they come in a little different form now, maybe, this way or that way. But it's the perfect job for somebody that wants to be working at 80 or 90.

—CNBC, May 7, 2018

LET'S SAY THAT when I turned 16, a genie appeared to me. And that genie says, "Warren, I'm going to give you the car of your choice. It'll be here tomorrow morning with a big bow tied on it. Brand-new. And it's all yours." Having heard all these genie stories, I would say, "What's the catch?" And the genie would answer, "There's only one catch. This is the last car you're ever going to get in your life. So it's got to last a lifetime."

Can you imagine, knowing it had to last a lifetime, what I would do with it? I would read the manual about five times. I would always keep it garaged. If there was the least little dent or scratch, I'd have it fixed right away because I wouldn't want it rusting....That's the position you're in concerning your mind and body. You only get one mind and body. And it's got to last a lifetime.

—*The Snowball*, 2008

If *Forbes* would put a list of the 400 oldest Americans and I was on that one—that's the list I really want to be on.

—CNBC, May 2, 2011

MEASURING SUCCESS

WHEN YOU GET to my age, you'll really measure success in life by how many of the people you want to have love you actually do love you. I know people who have a lot of money, and they get testimonial dinners and they get hospital wings named after them. But the truth is that nobody in the world loves them. If you get to my age in life and nobody thinks well of you, I don't care how big your bank account is, [your life] is a disaster.

—*Georgia Tech Alumni Magazine*, Winter 2003

LIVE LIKE A SIX-YEAR-OLD

I CHECKED THE actuarial tables, and the lowest death rate is among six-year-olds. So I decided to eat like a six-year-old. It's the safest course I can take.

—*Fortune*, February 25, 2015

I've reluctantly discarded the notion of my continuing to manage the portfolio after my death— abandoning my hope to give new meaning to the term "thinking outside the box."

—letter to Berkshire Hathaway shareholders, February 2008

RETIRING

I'M IN VERY good health, I love what I do and I'll go gaga someday and they'll yank me out of here.... My three kids are supposed to come in as a group and say, "You know, you're going gaga, Dad." I tell them if only one comes in, they're out of the will, so they have to come in as a group.

—CNBC, November 14, 2011

A FAIR SOCIETY

LET'S JUST ASSUME that it was 24 hours before you were born and a genie came to you and he said, "Herb, you look very promising and I've got a big problem. I've got to design the world in which you're going to live and ... I've decided ... it's too tough, *you* design it." ... You say, "I can design anything? ... There must be a catch." He says, "Well, there is a catch. You don't know whether you're going to be born black or white, rich or poor, male or female, infirm or able-bodied...."

You're going to participate in what I call the *ovarian lottery*. You're going to get one ball out of there and that is the most important thing that's ever going to happen to you in your life. That is going to control whether you're born here or in Afghanistan, or whether you're born with an IQ of 130 or an IQ of 70. . . .

I think that's a good way to look at social questions, because not knowing what ball you're going to get, you're going to want to design a system that includes lots of goods and services, because you're going to want people—on balance—to live well. And you're going to want it to produce more and more so your kids are going to live well and your grandchildren are going to live better than your kids, but you're also going to want a system that . . . does not leave behind a person who accidentally got the wrong ball.

University of Florida, October 15, 1998

Milestones

1930

- August 30: Warren Edward Buffett is born in Nebraska to Howard and Leila Buffett.

1941

- Buffett, 11, buys his first shares of stock with his sister Doris. After the shares initially lose value, WB sells them at a modest profit. Shortly after he sells them, the price per share goes up by more than 500 percent.

1942

- Buffett moves to Washington, DC, with his family when his father is elected to Congress.

1945

- Buffett invests $1,200 of savings in 40 acres of farmland, using money earned from delivering newspapers.

1947

- Buffett and a friend start a business enterprise. They purchase secondhand pinball machines, place them in local stores, including a barbershop, and collect the profits. Buffett sells the business.

- After graduating from high school, Buffett enrolls at the Wharton School in Pennsylvania. He complains that he knows more than his teachers.

1949

- Buffett transfers to the University of Nebraska–Lincoln, where he graduates after three years of college.

- Buffett reads Benjamin Graham's *The Intelligent Investor*, which he credits with teaching him the investment philosophies he uses throughout his life.

1950

- Buffett enrolls at Columbia University after learning that Graham is a professor there.

1951

- Buffett offers to work for Graham for free but is turned down. He graduates and returns to Omaha, where he begins dating Susan Thompson.

- Buffett invests $2,000 in a Sinclair service station, where he washes windshields on weekends. He loses the entire investment.

1952

- Buffett and Susan Thompson marry and have their first child, Susie.

1954

- Graham offers Buffett a job in his partnership, which he joins for a salary of $12,000 per year. The family moves to White Plains, New York, and Buffett becomes the partnership's star performer.

1956

- Graham retires and offers to make Buffett a partner in his business. Buffett, tired of New York and not interested in being a junior partner, turns him down.

- The family returns to Omaha, and Buffett decides to retire and live off the interest of his money.

- To earn enough money to retire, Buffett creates Buffett Associates, an investment partnership, with several friends. He then creates two more partnerships.

1957

- Buffett creates two more investment partnerships, bringing the total to five.

1961

- Buffett makes his first investment worth more than $1 million.

1962

- Buffett merges his partnerships into Buffett Partnerships, which is now worth around $7 million.

- Buffett begins to buy stock in the textile manufacturing company Berkshire Hathaway.

1964

- A fraud scandal brings the price of American Express stock down. Buffett begins buying shares, confident in the company and its long-term prospects.

1965

- Buffett invests heavily in the Walt Disney company, believing strongly in the future profitability of the company and the leadership qualities of Walt Disney himself, whom Buffett meets.

- Buffett takes control of Berkshire Hathaway and names a new president to run the company.

1969

- Buffett dissolves his various partnerships and distributes shares of stock in Berkshire Hathaway to his partners.

1970

- Berkshire Hathaway's earnings from insurance and various investments are more than 100 times as great as its textiles earnings. Buffett begins writing annual letters to Berkshire Hathaway shareholders.

1977

- Berkshire Hathaway acquires the Buffalo Evening News—while already having an interest in other newspapers, such as the *Washington Post*. This gives rise to antitrust claims that never materialize.

1983

- Berkshire Hathaway stock rises past $1,000 per share. Buffett's net worth reaches $620 million.

1985

- Buffett shuts down Berkshire textile mills after years of propping up the failing business.

1988

- Berkshire Hathaway begins buying over $1 billion of Coca-Cola stock

1990

- Berkshire Hathaway buys 10 percent of Wells Fargo.

1995

- Berkshire Hathaway acquires Helzberg Diamonds and RC Willey Home Furnishings.

1996

- Berkshire Hathaway fully acquires GEICO insurance company.

1997

- Berkshire Hathaway acquires Dairy Queen and Star Furniture, and invests in US Airways.

1998

- Berkshire Hathaway acquires General Re and Executive Jet.

1999

- Berkshire Hathaway acquires Jordan's Furniture and invests in MidAmerican Energy Holdings Company.

2000

- Buffett named the top money manager of the 20th century by the Carson Group.

- Berkshire Hathaway acquires Acme Building Brands, Shaw Industries, Benjamin Moore, and Johns Manville.

2004

- Buffett's wife, Susan, dies of a stroke.

2006

- Buffett announces his plan to give more than 80 percent of his fortune to five foundations, the largest part going to the Bill and Melinda Gates Foundation.

- Buffett marries Astrid Menks.

2006

- Buffett auctions off his 2001 Lincoln Town Car for charity.

2007

- Buffett announces that he is searching for a successor to run Berkshire Hathaway.

2008

- Buffett becomes the richest man in the world.

- With the stock market crashing, Buffett invests $5 billion in Goldman Sachs.

2010

- Buffett, Bill Gates, and Facebook CEO Mark Zuckerberg sign the Giving Pledge, promising to give away at least half of their accumulated wealth over time.

2011

- After Buffett argues that the taxes of wealthy Americans are too low, Barack Obama advocates the "Buffett Rule," a tax plan that would set a new tax rate for individuals earning more than $1 million per year.

2012

- Buffett discloses that he has stage 1 prostate cancer and will undergo radiation treatment. In September, he announces that his treatment cycle has concluded.

2013

- MidAmerican Energy Holdings Company, a subsidiary of Berkshire Hathaway, acquires two solar power plant projects in California for approximately $2 billion.

- Berkshire Hathaway and Brazilian firm 3G Capital Management partner to purchase Heinz for $28 billion.

- Berkshire Hathaway acquires shares in ExxonMobil Corporation.

2014

- Buffett and Quicken Loans partner to offer $1 billion to any fan who correctly guesses the final college basketball March Madness bracket. (No one wins.)

- The price of a single Berkshire Hathaway stock surpasses $200,000 for the first time.

- Berkshire Hathaway sells 245 million of its shares in UK grocery store chain Tesco, after Buffett calls the initial investment a mistake.

- Berkshire Hathaway purchases Duracell using $4.7 billion of Procter & Gamble stock.

2015

- Berkshire Hathaway and 3G Capital Management arrange a merger between Heinz, which the two firms own outright, and Kraft, which Berkshire holds shares in.

- Berkshire Hathaway purchases Precision Castparts, an aerospace manufacturer.

- Buffett endorses Hillary Clinton for president.

2016

- Berkshire Hathaway, usually averse to investing in the tech industry, purchases 10 million shares in Apple.

- Berkshire Hathaway begins buying stocks in several airlines, including Southwest, Delta, and American Airlines. Three years before, Buffett had argued that investing in airlines was a mistake. Investing watchdogs theorize that the acquisition of Precision Castparts made airline investment a safer bet for Berkshire.

- After presidential candidate Donald Trump claims that Buffett took a "massive" tax deduction, Buffett publicly states that he has paid income tax every year since 1944 and that he would gladly release his tax returns—unlike Trump.

2017

- Berkshire Hathaway sells about 90 percent of its shares in Walmart.

- Berkshire Hathaway sells about one-third of its stock in IBM after IBM stock prices fall over a number of years.

- Buffett criticizes the 2017 Better Care Reconciliation Act proposed by Senate Republican leaders for cutting the corporate tax rate. Buffett views corporate tax cuts as an unnecessary measure since corporations have done just as well under high tax rates as they have under lower ones.

2018

- Greg Abel and Ajit Jain join the Berkshire Hathaway board as vice chairs. Abel is appointed head of all Berkshire Hathaway's non–insurance related operations, while Jain oversees the insurance side of the business.

- *Forbes* ranks Buffett third (after Gates and Jeff Bezos) in its list of highest-earning billionaires.

- Berkshire Hathaway purchases approximately 75 million more shares in Apple.